HAR
BORO

in our time

in our time

the speeches that shaped the modern world

Hywel Williams

Quercus

Contents

Introduction 6

Éamon de Valera
'It is, indeed, hard for the strong to be just to the weak' 16 May 1945 8

Winston Churchill
'An iron curtain has descended across the Continent' 5 March 1946 13

George Marshall *'Our policy is directed not against any country or doctrine
but against hunger, poverty, desperation and chaos'* 5 June 1947 18

Jawaharlal Nehru
'A new star rises, the star of freedom in the east' 14 August 1947 21

David Ben-Gurion *'This is our native land, it is not as birds of passage that
we return to it'* 2 October 1947 28

Eleanor Roosevelt *'The basic problem confronting the world today . . .
is the preservation of human freedom'* 9 December 1948 33

Douglas MacArthur *'Old soldiers never die, they just fade away'* 19 April 1951 38

Nikita Khrushchev *'The cult of the individual brought about rude violation
of party democracy'* 25 February 1956 43

Aneurin Bevan *'The government resorted to epic weapons for squalid
and trivial ends'* 5 December 1956 48

Mao Zedong *'Let a hundred flowers blossom. Let a hundred schools of
thought contend'* 27 February 1957 53

Harold Macmillan *'The wind of change is blowing through this continent'*
3 February 1960 58

John F. Kennedy *'We stand today on the edge of a New Frontier'* 15 July 1960 63

John F. Kennedy *'Ask not what your country can do for you; ask what you can do
for your country'* 20 January 1961 68

John F. Kennedy *'Mankind must put an end to war – or war will put an end
to mankind'* 25 September 1961 73

Charles de Gaulle *'There is no independence imaginable for a country that
does not have its own nuclear weapon'* 15 February 1963 78

Martin Luther King, Jr *'I have a dream'* 28 August 1963 83

Harold Wilson *'The white heat of the technological revolution'* 1 October 1963 88

Nelson Mandela *'An ideal for which I am prepared to die'* 20 April 1964 93

Barry Goldwater *'Extremism in the defence of liberty is no vice . . .
moderation in the pursuit of justice is no virtue'* 16 July 1964 98

Martin Luther King, Jr *'The war in Vietnam is but a symptom of a far deeper malady
within the American spirit'* 4 April 1967 103

Julius Nyerere *'Socialism is an attitude of mind'* 10 April 1967 108

Gamal Abdel Nasser *'We are determined that the Palestine question will not be liquidated or forgotten'* 26 May 1967   113
'We are now ready to deal with the entire Palestine question' 29 May 1967   117

Richard Nixon *'North Vietnam cannot defeat or humiliate the United States. Only Americans can do that'* 3 November 1969   119

Richard Nixon *'Mistakes, yes. But for personal gain, never'* 9 August 1974   125

Pierre Trudeau *'The bringing home of our constitution marks the end of a long winter'* 17 April 1982   129

Neil Kinnock *'I warn you that you will have pain'* 7 June 1983   134
'We are democratic socialists. We care all the time' 15 May 1987   138

Ronald Reagan *'Isolationism never was and never will be an acceptable response to tyrannical governments'* 6 June 1984   140

Mario Cuomo *'For the love of God: Please, make this nation remember how futures are built'* 16 July 1984   145

Jesse Jackson *'Suffering breeds character. Character breeds faith. In the end, faith will not disappoint'* 18 July 1984   150

Richard von Weizsäcker *'Anyone who closes his eyes to the past is blind to the present'* 8 May 1985   155

Margaret Thatcher *'Let Europe be a family of nations . . . relishing our national identity no less than our common European endeavour'* 20 September 1988   160

Mikhail Gorbachev *'Freedom of choice is a universal principle to which there should be no exceptions'* 7 December 1988   165

Nelson Mandela *'A rainbow nation at peace with itself and the world'* 10 May 1994   170

Seamus Heaney *'The Ireland I now inhabit is one that these Irish contemporaries have helped to imagine'* 7 December 1995   175

Fidel Castro *'Socialism or death!'* 1 January 1999   180

Anita Roddick *'By putting our money where our heart is . . . we will mould the world into a kinder, more loving shape'* 27 November 1999   185

Tony Blair *'Our policies only succeed when the realism is as clear as the idealism'* 2 October 2001   190

Orhan Pamuk *'Whatever the country, freedom of thought and expression are universal human rights'* 25 April 2006   195

Kevin Rudd *'As of today, the time for denial, the time for delay, has at last come to an end'* 13 February 2008   200

Barack Obama *'We the people, in order to form a more perfect union'* 18 March 2008   205

Index   210

Acknowledgements/credits   215

Introduction

The oratory contained and discussed in this book reflects the currents of thought and alignments of power which created our contemporary world. Most of these speeches were delivered by politicians, national leaders who were intent on communicating the urgency of their message and the accuracy of their truth. Very many of them gained authority by democratic means and their words, spoken by and large at the very apex of their influence, reflect a career-long training in the art of eloquent persuasion. The speeches of Fidel Castro, Nikita Khrushchev and Chairman Mao reveal that dictatorial power may also seek to impress by demonstrating verbal skill – a technique which supplements the despot's habitual reliance on force. Generals MacArthur and Marshall show the military mind's analysis of geopolitics, while Eleanor Roosevelt and Martin Luther King, Jr display the commitment of the activist who gains moral authority and practical influence through dedication to a cause. The tide of events in war and peace, within nations and across frontiers, shapes the individual mind as well as the collective consciousness. Seamus Heaney and Orhan Pamuk show how literary art can reflect and also affect the conflicts within an individual artist's homeland, and their words track the impulsion of a writer's conscience towards the public domain.

This is therefore a book of many voices, one whose themes extend from the postwar era of reconstruction to the resurgence of a politicized Islam in the early 21st century. Many of these orators have been drawn to the question of national identity. Ben-Gurion in Israel, Nehru in India, Nyerere in Tanzania, and de Valera in Ireland: all were state-builders working in a culture whose origins were ancient. Thatcher's Britain and de Gaulle's France, by contrast, exemplify countries whose strong sense of a national culture was closely related to a long history of organized government. American political oratory, however, owes much of its zest to the feeling that the US is a civilization in the making rather than one whose history is behind it. Pierre Trudeau sought to ground Canadian national sentiment in a new constitution which respected diversity while also aspiring towards unity. Kevin Rudd's apology to Australia's indigenous peoples goes beyond introspection and invites a country to embark on a new phase of self-discovery. In all these instances, whether the nation-state was old or newer, oratory could pluck at the heart strings as well as appeal to the intellect when speaking of the roots of identity.

Nonetheless, the period which started in 1945, as Richard von Weizsäcker points out, records both victory and defeat for the notion of national self-determination. Western European nations were liberated from occupation, just as central and eastern European countries were to regain their freedom after 1989. But the past two generations have also recorded a rapid growth in the number of international organizations, such as the European Union, the United Nations, the Organization of African Unity, and the World Trade Organization. Their competence has often been tested and their authority criticized, but their existence is testimony to an ever-widening dimension in ethics, politics and economics. International issues involving human rights, disarmament, globalized capitalism and terrorism have given a new range to the oratory of those who seek to change the world by influencing our opinions. Anita Roddick's anger at multi-national companies, Tony Blair's aspiration to a renewed world order, and Nelson Mandela's message of multi-racial tolerance all touch on these wider themes which transcend the narrower lives of nations.

By the end of our period few public figures buttressed their speeches with quotations from the ancients, as Harold Macmillan liked to do. Attention was now gained by pithier means. But the elements that go to make a great speech hardly change at all, as the history of rhetoric shows. It was first formalised as a subject in classical Rome during the first centuries BC and AD, and from the middle ages to the renaissance a study of rhetoric was basic to the educational curriculum. Rote-learning led to an emphasis on mere technique, and 'rhetorical' acquired its pejorative modern meaning. Nowadays, we like our speakers to show authenticity rather than just follow the rules about how to vary pitch and tone. But without such skills a speaker can lose an audience and, thereby, the argument. The appeal to mind and heart through the order of thought and the clarification of feeling is the basis of great oratory. One person stands alone before the many, experiences the anticipation, and starts to speak. This is the grand continuity, and these are the voices that mattered in our time.

HYWEL WILLIAMS, 2008

'It is, indeed, hard for the strong to be just to the weak'

Éamon de Valera
(1882–1975)

IRELAND'S PRIME MINISTER EXPLAINS HIS GOVERNMENT'S POLICY OF NEUTRALITY;
ADDRESS ON RADIO ÉIREANN, 16 MAY 1945

'It is, indeed, hard for the strong to be just to the weak'

Winston Churchill's attack on the Irish government's neutrality during the Second World War formed part of a speech marking 'Victory in Europe' and had been broadcast across the world. In it he contrasted 'the action of Mr de Valera' with the 'instinct of thousands of Southern Irishmen who hastened to the battle-front to prove their ancient valour'. Irish neutrality, he maintained, had exposed Britain to additional danger during the Battle of the Atlantic, when German U-boats attacked the convoys travelling from North America to the UK. The inability to use Irish ports or to benefit from their refuelling facilities had reduced the range and effectiveness of British ships escorting the transatlantic convoys: 'if it had not been for the loyalty and friendship of Northern Ireland, we would have been forced to come to close quarters with Mr de Valera or perish forever from the earth.'

The ports in question were the deep-water bases at Cobh (Queenstown) and Berehaven on Ireland's southern coast, and Lough Swilly in the northwest. Known previously as the 'Treaty Ports', they had been retained as sovereign bases by the UK government following Ireland's 1922 partition and the creation of the Irish Free State. Neville Chamberlain returned the bases to Ireland in 1938, a move Churchill regarded as characteristically short-sighted, but which the Irish government regarded as vital to protect its neutrality in the event of war. Britain's exclusion from the two southern port facilities was especially significant since they were some 200 miles (320 km) further out into the Atlantic than any other naval bases available to its forces. Losses in this theatre of war were especially heavy

ÉAMON DE VALERA (1882–1975)

1913 Joins Irish Volunteers, a military organization backing Home Rule.

1916 Participates in Easter Rising against British rule and sentenced to death before a stay of execution.

1917 Becomes president of Sinn Féin.

1918 Sinn Féin wins majority of Irish seats in the British general election.

Jan 1919 An Irish parliament (Dáil) is formed but not recognized by the British.

1919–21 Irish War of Independence.

Oct–Dec 1921 Treaty negotiations in London, not attended by de Valera, agree to independence for 26 of Ireland's 32 counties.

1922–37 Constitution of the Irish Free State.

1922–3 Supports the anti-Treaty IRA in Irish Civil War; arrested and interned until 1924.

1926 Founds republican party, Fianna Fáil.

1932 Forms his first Free State government.

1937 New Irish constitution enacted.

1937 Becomes Ireland's first taoiseach (prime minister); in office 1937–48, 1951–4, 1957–9.

1949 Ireland becomes a republic and leaves the British Commonwealth.

for the British, with 245 vessels sunk by German U-boats between July and October 1940. Britain's occupation of Iceland in the same year, however, provided the Allies with additional bases for their Atlantic operations.

De Valera's dignified response is no less powerful for being so subtle. He hints that Britain's espousal of the rights of smaller nations is hypocritical, and Churchill is treated with a delicate irony. The imaginative shift portraying a German-occupied England, and the anticipated English reaction to being partitioned, is exquisitely done. As de Valera concedes, his reaction would have been less poised in earlier years, and the speech expresses a veiled regret at his own role in shedding blood. He had dissociated himself from the Anglo-Irish Treaty agreed in 1921 largely because it granted Ireland dominion status within the British Commonwealth, rather than full independence as a republic. The arrangements concerning the Treaty Ports formed part of a constitutional settlement which, for de Valera, limited Ireland's ability to pursue an independent foreign policy. As Colonial Secretary in 1921–2, Churchill had been one of the treaty's chief negotiators, so the issue he had now chosen to disinter was one with which he was very familiar.

Certain newspapers have been very persistent in looking for my answer to Mr Churchill's recent broadcast. I know the kind of answer I am expected to make . . .

I know the reply I would have given a quarter of a century ago. But I have deliberately decided that that is not the reply I shall make tonight. I shall strive not to be guilty of adding any fuel to the flames of hatred or passion which, if continued to be fed, promise to burn up whatever is left by the war of decent human feeling in Europe.

'I shall strive not to be guilty of adding any fuel to the flames of hatred or passion'

Allowances can be made for Mr Churchill's statement, however unworthy, in the first flush of his victory. No such excuse could be found for me in this quieter atmosphere. There are, however, some things which it is my duty to say . . .

Mr Churchill makes it clear that, in certain circumstances, he would have violated our neutrality and that he would justify his actions by Britain's necessity. It seems strange to me that Mr Churchill does not see that this, if accepted, would mean that Britain's necessity would become a moral code and that when this necessity became sufficiently great, other people's rights were not to count.

It is quite true that other great powers believe in this same code – in their own regard – and have behaved in accordance with it. That is precisely why we have the disastrous succession of wars – World War no. 1 and World War no. 2 – and shall it be World War no. 3?

Surely Mr Churchill must see that, if his contention be admitted in our regard, a like justification can be framed for similar acts of aggression elsewhere and no small nation adjoining a great power could ever hope to be permitted to go its own way in peace.

It is, indeed, fortunate that Britain's necessity did not reach the point when Mr Churchill would have acted. All credit to him that he successfully resisted the temptation . . . It is, indeed, hard for the strong to be just to the weak, but acting justly always has its rewards.

By resisting his temptation in this instance, Mr Churchill, instead of adding another horrid chapter to the already bloodstained record of the relations between England and this country, has advanced the cause of international morality . . .

'No small nation adjoining a great power could ever hope to be permitted to go its own way in peace'

That Mr Churchill should be irritated when our neutrality stood in the way of what he thought he vitally needed, I understand, but that he or any thinking person in Britain or elsewhere should fail to see the reason for our neutrality, I find it hard to conceive.

I would like to put a hypothetical question . . . Suppose Germany had won the war, had invaded and occupied England, and that after a long lapse of time and many bitter struggles she was finally brought to acquiesce in admitting England's right to freedom, and let England go, but not the whole of England, all but, let us say, the six southern counties.

These six southern counties, those, let us suppose, commanding the entrance to the narrow seas, Germany had singled out and insisted on holding herself with a view to weakening England as a whole and maintaining the security of her own communications through the Straits of Dover.

Let us suppose, further, that after all this had happened Germany was engaged in a great war in which she could show that she was on the side of the freedom of a number of small nations. Would Mr Churchill as an Englishman who believed that his own nation had as good a right to freedom as any other – not freedom for a part merely, but freedom for the whole – would he, whilst Germany still maintained the partition of his country and occupied six counties of it, would he lead this partitioned England to join with Germany in a crusade? I do not think Mr Churchill would.

Would he think the people of partitioned England an object of shame if they stood neutral in such circumstances? I do not think Mr Churchill would.

Mr Churchill is proud of Britain's stand alone, after France had fallen and before America entered the war. Could he not find in his heart the generosity to acknowledge that there is a small nation that stood alone, not for one year or two, but for several hundred years against aggression; that endured spoliations, famines, massacres in endless succession; that was clubbed many times into insensibility, but that each time on returning consciousness, took up the fight anew; a small nation that could never be got to accept defeat and has never surrendered her soul?

> *'A small nation that stood alone, not for one year or two, but for several hundred years against aggression'*

Mr Churchill is justly proud of his nation's perseverance against heavy odds. But we in this island are still prouder of our people's perseverance for freedom through all the centuries. We of our time have played our part in that perseverance, and we have pledged ourselves to the dead generations who have preserved intact for us this glorious heritage, that we too will strive to be faithful to the end, and pass on this tradition unblemished.

Many a time in the past there appeared little hope except that hope to which Mr Churchill referred, that by standing fast a time would come when, to quote his own words, 'the tyrant would make some ghastly mistake which would alter the whole balance of the struggle.'

> *'I have had a vision of a nobler and better ending, better for both our peoples and for the future of mankind'*

I sincerely trust, however, that it is not thus our ultimate unity and freedom will be achieved, though as a younger man I confess I prayed even for that . . .

In latter years I have had a vision of a nobler and better ending, better for both our peoples and for the future of mankind. For that I have now been long working. I regret that it is not to this nobler purpose that Mr Churchill is lending his hand rather than by the abuse of a people who have done him no wrong, trying to find in a crisis like the present excuse for continuing the injustice of the mutilation of our country . . .

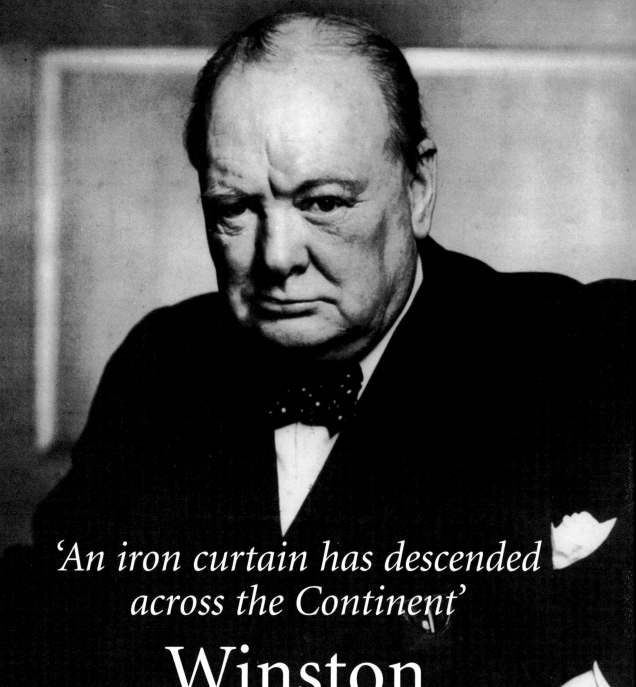

'An iron curtain has descended across the Continent'

Winston Churchill

(1874–1965)

BRITAIN'S WARTIME PRIME MINISTER WARNS OF THE DANGERS OF
A DIVIDED EUROPE; LECTURE AT WESTMINSTER COLLEGE,
FULTON, MISSOURI, 5 MARCH 1946

At the time of delivering this speech, Britain's wartime prime minister, Winston Churchill, was serving as leader of the opposition following the Conservative Party's defeat in the 1945 general election. The sonorous phraseology and broad historical sweep which had typified Churchill's wartime oratory remained undimmed and his speech marked the effective beginning of the Cold War. Broadcast by newsreel across the English-speaking world, the delivery of these words crystallized the significance of what was happening in Europe. The continent's division into two armed camps whose ethical and political values were fundamentally opposed to each other is described graphically, and the phrase 'iron curtain', here introduced for the first time, entered into common currency as a result. The man who had warned his country against appeasement of fascism in the 1930s was now resuming his role as prophet. Churchill is describing not just the reality of communist power in Europe but also the range of its totalitarian ambitions and the effectiveness of its subversive methods. The vision is a global one and the need to enrol the United States in what would be an Asian as well as a European struggle explains why Churchill deemed the American Midwest a good place in which to sound this particular trumpet.

Evocation of threat, however, is not the speech's sole keynote. Political imaginativeness, audacious planning and generosity of spirit are also present. Churchill the social progressive advocates welfare and government action to protect individuals and families from need and starvation. Democracy, he recognizes, has to prove its superiority to communism in this regard. Success in this area was needed to strengthen what Churchill

WINSTON CHURCHILL (1874-1965)

1900 Elected MP (Conservative) for Oldham, Lancashire.

1904 Joins Liberal Party.

1906 Elected MP (Liberal) for Manchester North-West.

1908 Appointed president of the Board of Trade; elected MP (Liberal) for Dundee.

1910 Appointed home secretary.

1911–15 Serves as first lord of the Admiralty.

1917–19 Minister of munitions.

1919–21 Secretary of state for war and air.

1921–2 Secretary of state for the colonies.

1922 Loses Dundee seat in the general election which returns a Conservative government.

1924 Elected MP for Epping, sitting initially as an independent, then as a Conservative.

1924–9 Chancellor of the exchequer.

1939 First Lord of the admiralty.

1940–5, 1951–5 Prime minister.

called 'the sinews of peace' and to consolidate thereby the wider political freedoms enjoyed in the democratic West.

In 1946 Churchill was still clinging to his ardent belief in the British empire, despite the obviousness of its imminent dissolution. Formed in the high noon of his country's late Victorian imperialism, he found it inconceivable that Britain should be anything other than an independent power. But his political education as an imperial statesman also meant that he thought naturally in terms that went beyond the confines of the nation state. It was this experience that equipped him to describe so imaginatively the immediate need of the postwar world: supranational institutions which transcended narrowly exclusive definitions of sovereignty and citizenship. After the fall of France in May 1940 he had proposed a joint Franco-British citizenship, and this speech's contemplation of British-American citizenship was similarly audacious. Speaking in Zurich in September 1946, Churchill would advocate 'a kind of United States of Europe', an entity that he thought should exist alongside the British empire and the Commonwealth. Security needs, as described in Fulton, Missouri, dictated large power blocs as a counterpoise to the USSR, and the idea of a balance of power exercised between a number of independent states was deemed obsolete and dangerous. At the beginning of his eighth decade Winston Churchill remained both a visionary and a realist.

The United States stands at this time at the pinnacle of world power. It is a solemn moment for the American democracy. For with primacy in power is also joined an awe-inspiring accountability to the future . . . Opportunity is here now, clear and shining for both our countries . . . It is necessary that constancy of mind, persistency of purpose, and the grand simplicity of decision shall guide and rule the conduct of the English-speaking peoples in peace as they did in war . . .

What then is the overall strategic concept which we should inscribe today? It is nothing less than the safety and welfare, the freedom and progress, of all the homes and families of all the men and women in all the lands . . . To give security to these countless homes, they must be shielded from the two giant marauders, war and tyranny . . . The awful ruin of Europe, with all its vanished glories, and of large parts of Asia, glares us in the eyes . . .

'Opportunity is here now, clear and shining for both our countries'

When I stand here this quiet afternoon I shudder to visualize what is actually happening to millions now and what is going to happen in this period when famine stalks the earth . . .

The United Nations Organization must immediately begin to be equipped with an international armed force . . . I propose that each of the Powers and States should be invited to delegate a certain number of air squadrons to the service of the world organization. These squadrons would be trained and prepared in their own countries, but would move around in rotation from one country to another . . . They would not be required to act against their own nation, but in other respects they would be directed by the world organization . . .

We cannot be blind to the fact that the liberties enjoyed by individual citizens throughout the British Empire are not valid in a considerable number of countries . . . In these states . . . power is exercised without restraint, either by dictators or by compact oligarchies operating through a privileged party and a political police . . .

'Eventually there may come – I feel eventually there will come – the principle of common citizenship'

Neither the sure prevention of war, nor the continuous rise of world organization, will be gained without . . . the fraternal association of the English-speaking peoples. This means a special relationship between the British Commonwealth and Empire and the United States. Fraternal association requires . . . the continuance of the intimate relationship between our military advisers, leading to common study of potential dangers, the similarity of weapons and manuals of instruction, and to the interchange of officers and cadets at technical colleges. The United States has already a Permanent Defence Agreement with the Dominion of Canada . . . This principle should be extended to all British Commonwealths with full reciprocity . . . Eventually there may come – I feel eventually there will come – the principle of common citizenship . . .

A shadow has fallen upon the scenes so lately lighted by the Allied victory . . . From Stettin in the Baltic to Trieste in the Adriatic, an iron curtain has descended across the Continent. Behind that line lie all the capitals of the ancient states of Central and Eastern Europe. Warsaw, Berlin, Prague, Vienna, Budapest, Belgrade, Bucharest and Sofia, all these famous cities and the populations around them lie in what I must call the Soviet sphere, and all are subject in one form or another, not only to Soviet influence but to a very high and, in many cases, increasing measure of control from Moscow. An attempt is being made by the Russians in Berlin to build up a quasi-Communist Party in their zone of Occupied Germany by showing special favours to groups of left-wing German leaders. This is certainly not the Liberated Europe we fought to build up. Nor is it one which contains the essentials of permanent peace.

'The old doctrine of the balance of power is unsound'

The safety of the world requires a new unity in Europe, from which no nation should be permanently outcast. It is from the quarrels of the strong parent races in Europe that the world wars we have witnessed, or which occurred in former times, have sprung. Surely we should work with conscious purpose for a grand pacification of Europe.

In front of the iron curtain which lies across Europe are other causes of anxiety. In a great number of countries . . . communist fifth columns are established and work in complete unity and absolute obedience to the decisions they receive from the communist centre.

I do not believe that Soviet Russia desires war. What they desire is the fruits of war and the indefinite expansion of their power and doctrines. From what I have seen of our Russian friends and Allies during the war, I am convinced that there is nothing they admire so much as strength, and there is nothing for which they have less respect than weakness, especially military weakness. For that reason the old doctrine of the balance of power is unsound. We cannot afford . . . to work on narrow margins, offering temptations to a trial of strength. If the Western Democracies stand together in strict adherence to the principles of the United Nations Charter, their influence for furthering those principles will be immense . . . If however they become divided . . . and if these all-important years are allowed to slip away then indeed catastrophe may overwhelm us all.

'I have had a vision of a nobler and better ending, better for both our peoples and for the future of mankind'

Let no man underrate the abiding power of the British Empire and Commonwealth. Because you see the 46 millions in our island harassed about their food supply . . . or because we have difficulty in restarting our industry and export trade . . . do not suppose that we shall not come through these dark years of privation as we have come through the glorious years of agony, or that half a century from now, you will not see 70 or 80 millions of Britons . . . united in defence of our traditions, our way of life, and of the world causes which you and we espouse. If we adhere faithfully to the Charter of the United Nations and walk forward in sedate and sober strength . . . if all British moral and material forces and convictions are joined with your own in fraternal association, the high-roads of the future will be clear, not only for us but for all, not only for our time, but for a century to come.

'Our policy is directed not against any country or doctrine but against hunger, poverty, desperation and chaos'

George Marshall

(1880–1959)

THE US SECRETARY OF STATE OUTLINES THE EUROPEAN RECOVERY PROGRAMME;
SPEECH DELIVERED AT HARVARD UNIVERSITY, 5 JUNE 1947

'Our policy is directed not against any country or doctrine but against hunger, poverty, desperation and chaos'

The Marshall Plan was the brain-child of the US State Department. Dean Acheson, then under-secretary of state, was a major influence on the policy, as were two officials, Charles Bohlen, who wrote Marshall's speech, and George Kennan. During the four years of its operation until 1952 a total of 13 billion dollars' worth of economic aid and technical assistance was made available by the US to the participating countries: Austria, Belgium, Denmark, France, West Germany, the UK, Greece, Iceland, Ireland, Italy, Luxembourg, the Netherlands, Norway, Sweden, Switzerland and Turkey. The USSR and its satellite states in Central and Eastern Europe refused to participate, seeing the programme as an American ruse to exert control over their internal affairs. Western Europe's economic integration, however, was advanced by the Plan's removal of national tariff barriers, and the Organization for European Economic Cooperation, the institution devised to allocate the aid money, influenced the thinking of Europe's political integrationists.

Northwestern Europe's harsh winter in 1946–7 aggravated an already acute situation. Roads, railways and bridges, as well as most urban centres, had suffered aerial bombardment. Damage to infrastructure meant that smaller towns were isolated, and Eastern Europe's food surpluses were trapped behind the Iron Curtain. Germany's industrial base in coal and steel, vital for the entire European economy, was wrecked, and the Allies had imposed postwar restrictions on West Germany's heavy industrial capacity. Some of these constraints would be lifted, but the dismantling of German manufacturing businesses, including steel plants, would continue into the late 1940s.

With the US now alert to French and Italian communist threats, the Plan formed part of the State Department's newly embraced doctrine of 'containment', a policy which tried to stop

GEORGE MARSHALL (1880–1959)

1901 Graduates from Virginia Military Institute.

1917 Serves in France with the 1st Infantry Division during the the First World War.

1918 Joins headquarters of American Expeditionary Forces, the US's military force in Europe.

1936 Promoted to rank of brigadier-general.

1939 Promoted to full general; becomes US Army's chief of staff.

1944 Promoted to 5-star rank as general of the army, the US Army's highest rank.

1944–5 Coordinates Allied operations in Europe and the Pacific.

1945–7 Sent by President Truman to China: attempts unsuccessfully to broker peace in the country's civil war.

1947 Appointed US secretary of state.

1950–1 Secretary of defence.

1953 Awarded Nobel Peace Prize for the Marshall Plan.

the spread of Soviet influence to non-communist countries. Greece and Turkey, both exposed to communist aggression, were already receiving US economic and military assistance under the terms of the so-called Truman Doctrine, announced by President Harry S. Truman on 12 March 1947.

The aid money was mostly used to buy US goods, especially food, fuel and materiel for infrastructure development. This met a real American need for export-led demand. Geared to a war economy from 1942 to 1945, American factories had produced the fastest economic growth in US history. Peacetime required new markets and the Plan boosted postwar American consumerism.

By the early 1950s, the aggregate Gross National Product of countries participating in the Plan had risen by more than 30 per cent compared to pre-war levels; industrial production by 40 per cent. West Germany took longer to recover, and sceptics of the Marshall Plan adduced the country's reduction in economic regulations as the reason for its eventual phenomenal success.

The Plan's example encouraged the growth of an entire aid industry from the 1950s onwards. International organizations administering aid would also attract criticism of waste and corruption. But the principle outlined by Marshall in his speech had by then entered into the mainstream thinking of Western leaders: 'hunger, poverty, desperation and chaos' required the intervention of the powerful and prosperous.

I need not tell you, gentlemen, that the world situation is very serious. I think one difficulty is that the problem is one of such enormous complexity that the very mass of facts presented to the public by press and radio make it exceedingly difficult for the man in the street to reach a clear appraisement of the situation.

Furthermore, the people of this country are distant from the troubled areas of the earth and it is hard for them to comprehend the plight and consequent reactions of the long-suffering peoples, and the effect of those reactions on their governments in connection with our efforts to promote peace in the world.

'The rehabilitation of the economic structure of Europe quite evidently will require a much longer time and greater effort than had been foreseen'

In considering the requirements for the rehabilitation of Europe, the physical loss of life, the visible destruction of cities, factories, mines and railroads was correctly estimated. But it has become obvious during recent months that this visible destruction was probably less serious

'Our policy is directed not against any country or doctrine but against hunger, poverty, desperation and chaos'

than the dislocation of the entire fabric of the European economy. Machinery has fallen into disrepair or is entirely obsolete. Under the arbitrary and destructive Nazi rule, virtually every possible enterprise was geared into the German war machine. Long-standing commercial ties, private institutions, banks, insurance companies and shipping companies disappeared, through loss of capital, absorption through nationalization or by simple destruction. In many countries, confidence in the local currency has been severely shaken. The rehabilitation of the economic structure of Europe quite evidently will require a much longer time and greater effort than had been foreseen.

There is a phase of this matter which is both interesting and serious. The farmer has always produced the foodstuffs to exchange with the city dweller for the other necessities of life. This division of labour is the basis of modern civilization. At the present time it is threatened with breakdown.

'A very serious situation is rapidly developing which bodes no good for the world'

The town and city industries are not producing adequate goods to exchange with the food-producing farmer. Raw materials and fuel are in short supply. Machinery is lacking or worn out. The farmer or the peasant cannot find the goods for sale which he desires to purchase. So the sale of his farm produce for money which he cannot use seems to him an unprofitable transaction. He, therefore, has withdrawn many fields from crop cultivation and is using them for grazing. He feeds more grain to stock and finds for himself and his family an ample supply of food, however short he may be on clothing and the other ordinary gadgets of civilization.

Meanwhile, people in the cities are short of food and fuel. So the governments are forced to use their foreign money and credits to procure these necessities abroad. This process exhausts funds which are urgently needed for reconstruction. Thus a very serious situation is rapidly developing which bodes no good for the world. The modern system of the division of labour upon which the exchange of products is based is in danger of breaking down.

The truth of the matter is that Europe's requirements for the next three or four years of foreign food and other essential products – principally from America – are so much greater than her present ability to pay that she must have additional help or face economic, social and political deterioration of a very grave character.

The remedy lies in breaking the vicious circle and restoring the confidence of the European people in the economic future of their own countries and of Europe as a whole. The manufacturer and the farmer . . . must be able and willing to exchange their products for currencies the continuing value of which is not open to question.

Aside from the demoralizing effect on the world at large and the possibilities of disturbances arising as a result of the desperation of the people concerned, the consequences to the economy of the United States should be apparent to all. It is logical that the United States should do whatever it is able to do to assist in the return of normal economic health in the world, without which there can be no political stability and no assured peace.

'The United States should do whatever it is able to do to assist in the return of normal economic health in the world'

Our policy is directed not against any country or doctrine but against hunger, poverty, desperation and chaos. Its purpose should be the revival of a working economy in the world so as to permit the emergence of political and social conditions in which free institutions can exist. Such assistance, I am convinced, must not be on a piecemeal basis as various crises develop.

Any government that is willing to assist in the task of recovery will find cooperation, I am sure, on the part of the United States government. Any government which manoeuvres to block the recovery of other countries cannot expect help from us. Furthermore, governments, political parties or groups which seek to perpetuate human misery in order to profit therefrom politically or otherwise will encounter the opposition of the United States.

It is already evident that, before the United States government can proceed much further in its efforts to alleviate the situation . . . there must be some agreement among the countries of Europe. It would be neither fitting nor efficacious for this government to undertake to draw up unilaterally a programme designed to place Europe on its feet economically. This is the business of the Europeans. The role of this country should consist of friendly aid in the drafting of a European programme and of later support of such a programme so far as it may be practical for us to do so. The programme should be a joint one, agreed to by a number, if not all European nations.

'Political passion and prejudice should have no part'

An essential part of any successful action on the part of the United States is an understanding on the part of the people of America of the character of the problem and the remedies to be applied. Political passion and prejudice should have no part. With foresight, and a willingness on the part of our people to face up to the vast responsibility which history has clearly placed upon our country, the difficulties I have outlined can and will be overcome.

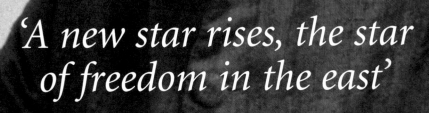

'A *new star rises, the star of freedom in the east*'

Jawaharlal Nehru

(1889–1964)

INDIA'S FIRST PRIME MINISTER MARKS HIS COUNTRY'S INDEPENDENCE;
SPEECH TO THE CONSTITUENT ASSEMBLY, NEW DELHI, 14 AUGUST 1947

The influence of his English education is clearly evident in the speech delivered by Jawaharlal Nehru, India's first prime minister. Phrases such as 'tryst with destiny' and 'the stroke of the midnight hour' show a familiarity with the cadences of the language and a capacity to use it to poetic as well as dramatic effect. Born the son of a rich lawyer, Nehru wrote and spoke as the member of an Anglophone elite, and he had learnt English, as well as Hindi and Sanskrit, while growing up at the family home in Allahabad. Nehru's Westernization was not just a matter of speech and manner. The insurgent style of anti-colonialism he adopted in the 1920s owed much to the revolutionary agitation of contemporary Europe. Like his great mentor Mahatma Gandhi, he espoused India's self-reliance and attached himself to her native customs, practising yoga and reading the *Bhagavad Gita*. But the adoption of these cultural practices coexisted uneasily with his attachment to socialism, a European creed and one which showed the profound impact of the West on his intellectual development.

Part of the speech's fascination lies in the way it reveals these different aspects of Nehru's mind and personality. These are the words of a leader who was born to command, a patrician who enjoins his people to 'incessant striving' in order to be worthy of India. Nehru's father was an influential figure within the Indian National Congress, the political party which provided the country with its new establishment. Family patronage helped his early political career and, although he distrusted dynasticism, Nehru's successors among India's prime ministers include his daughter Indira and grandson Rajiv. Nonetheless, long periods of imprisonment by the British authorities, from 1931 to 1935 and again from 1942 to 1945, on account of his incitement to mass rebellion, earned Nehru the right to lead and gained him the adulation of the Congress masses.

JAWAHARLAL NEHRU (1889–1964)

1905 Leaves India for England and an education at Harrow, Trinity College, Cambridge, and the Inner Temple, London.

1924–6 President of the Municipal Corporation, Allahabad; pioneers schemes to improve education, health, sanitation and employment rates.

1928 Rejects his father's 'Nehru Report' which urges India's 'dominion status' within the British empire.

1929 Elected president of the Indian National Congress (INC), with the party now committed to full independence.

1936 Re-elected president of the INC; urges the party's adoption of socialism.

1942–5 Imprisoned by the British after urging rebellion in support of the Congress call for the British to 'quit India' in an immediate transfer of power.

1947–64 Prime minister of India.

'The greatest man of our generation' and 'father of our nation' Nehru alludes to is Gandhi, and the account of India's 'trackless centuries' echoes the Mahatma's tradition-based nationalism. But this is also a call to progressive politics issued by a secular-minded man to a deeply religious society. Nehru, quite significantly, makes no reference to India's gods. It was the Muslim–Hindu divide which explained why the pledge to achieve India's independence was redeemed only 'substantially'. The plan to partition India, released by the departing British on 3 June 1947, had been rushed through, and by August a Muslim-dominated state of Pakistan had been created, a country of two wings separated by more than 1000 miles (1600 km) of Indian territory. History's greatest population transfer involved some 18 million Muslims, Hindus and Sikhs, and the interreligious strife which spread through the Punjab, Bengal and Delhi claimed the lives of hundreds of thousands. This was the bloodiest inauguration possible. But in the decades following independence, and despite the persistence of religious violence, Nehru's words still stood as a reference point and a reminder of what India might yet become.

Long years ago we made a tryst with destiny, and now the time comes when we shall redeem our pledge, not wholly or in full measure, but very substantially.

At the stroke of the midnight hour, when the world sleeps, India will awake to life and freedom. A moment comes, which comes but rarely in history, when we step out from the old to the new, when an age ends, and when the soul of a nation, long suppressed, finds utterance.

It is fitting that at this solemn moment we take the pledge of dedication to the service of India and her people and to the still larger cause of humanity.

'At the stroke of the midnight hour, when the world sleeps, India will awake to life and freedom'

At the dawn of history India started on her unending quest, and trackless centuries are filled with her striving and the grandeur of her successes and her failures. Through good and ill fortune alike she has never lost sight of that quest or forgotten the ideals which gave her strength. We end today a period of ill fortune and India discovers herself again . . .

Freedom and power bring responsibility. The responsibility rests upon this assembly, a sovereign body representing the sovereign people of India. Before the birth of freedom we have endured all the pains of labour and our hearts are heavy with the memory of this sorrow. Some of those pains continue even now. Nevertheless, the past is over and it is the future that beckons to us now.

That future is not one of ease or resting but of incessant striving so that we may fulfil the pledges we have so often taken and the one we shall take today. The service of India means the service of the millions who suffer. It means the ending of poverty and ignorance and disease and inequality of opportunity.

The ambition of the greatest man of our generation has been to wipe every tear from every eye. That may be beyond us, but as long as there are tears and suffering . . . our work will not be over.

And so we have to labour and to work, and work hard, to give reality to our dreams. Those dreams are for India, but they are also for the world, for all the nations and peoples are too closely knit together today for anyone of them to imagine that it can live apart.

'As long as there are tears and suffering, our work will not be over'

Peace has been said to be indivisible; so is freedom, so is prosperity now, and so also is disaster in this one world that can no longer be split into isolated fragments.

To the people of India, whose representatives we are, we make an appeal to join us with faith and confidence in this great adventure. This is no time for petty and destructive criticism, no time for ill will or blaming others. We have to build the noble mansion of free India where all her children may dwell.

The appointed day has come – the day appointed by destiny – and India stands forth again, after long slumber and struggle, awake, vital, free and independent. The past clings on to us still in some measure and we have to do much before we redeem the pledges we have so often taken. Yet the turning point is past, and history begins anew for us, the history which we shall live and act and others will write about.

'We have to build the noble mansion of free India where all her children may dwell'

It is a fateful moment for us in India, for all Asia and for the world. A new star rises, the star of freedom in the east, a new hope comes into being, a vision long cherished materializes. May the star never set and that hope never be betrayed! . . .

On this day our first thoughts go to the architect of this freedom, the father of our nation, who, embodying the old spirit of India, held aloft the torch of freedom and lighted up the darkness that surrounded us. We have often been unworthy followers of his and have strayed from his message, but not only we but succeeding generations will remember this message and bear the imprint in their hearts of this great son of India, magnificent in his faith and strength and courage and humility. We shall never allow that torch of freedom to be blown out, however high the wind or stormy the tempest.

Our next thoughts must be of the unknown volunteers and soldiers of freedom who, without praise or reward, have served India even unto death.

We think also of our brothers and sisters who have been cut off from us by political boundaries and who unhappily cannot share at present in the freedom that has come. They are of us and will remain of us whatever may happen, and we shall be sharers in their good and ill fortune alike.

'We shall never allow that torch of freedom to be blown out'

The future beckons to us. Whither do we go and what shall be our endeavour? To bring freedom and opportunity to the common man, to the peasants and workers of India; to fight and end poverty and ignorance and disease; to build up a prosperous, democratic and progressive nation, and to create social, economic and political institutions which will ensure justice and fullness of life to every man and woman.

We have hard work ahead. There is no resting for any one of us till we redeem our pledge in full, till we make all the people of India what destiny intended them to be.

We are citizens of a great country, on the verge of bold advance, and we have to live up to that high standard. All of us, to whatever religion we may belong, are equally the children of India with equal rights, privileges and obligations. We cannot encourage communalism or narrow-mindedness, for no nation can be great whose people are narrow in thought or action.

To the nations and peoples of the world we send greetings and pledge ourselves to cooperate with them in furthering peace, freedom and democracy.

And to India, our much-loved motherland, the ancient, the eternal and the ever-new, we pay our reverent homage and we bind ourselves afresh to her service.

This is our native land; it is not as birds of passage that we return to it'

David Ben-Gurion

(1886–1973)

ISRAEL'S SOON-TO-BE FIRST PRIME MINISTER ADDRESSES THE ELECTED
ASSEMBLY OF PALESTINE JEWRY, JERUSALEM, 2 OCTOBER 1947

'This is our native land; it is not as birds of passage that we return to it'

The Mandate for Palestine was granted to Britain by the League of Nations after the Treaty of Sèvres (10 August 1920) split up the Middle Eastern territories of the Ottoman empire following its defeat in the First World War. The area for which Britain became responsible extended eastwards as far as the boundary of Britain's equivalent Mandate for Mesopotamia (Iraq). The Mandates for Lebanon to the north and for Syria to the northeast were administered by France. Britain's 'Palestine' included Transjordan, which it effectively ran as a separate area, while it recognized the territory to the west of the River Jordan as Palestine proper. The Balfour Declaration (2 November 1917), issued by the British foreign secretary A.J. Balfour, stated that the UK government favoured the establishment in Palestine of 'a national home for the Jewish people' and the clauses of Britain's Mandate empowered it to facilitate Jewish immigration to the region.

The Jewish Agency for Palestine, here addressed by Ben-Gurion, administered the local Jewish community and was officially recognized by the British. That community's numbers increased greatly as Jews fled European fascism, but the British government's 'white paper' of 1939 introduced controversial immigration quotas. Discontent with the Mandate led to the formation of militant Jewish organizations such as Irgun, which in 1946 blew up the King David Hotel in Jerusalem, the British administration's headquarters. By the time this speech was delivered, Britain had announced that it wanted to end the Mandate. Despite Ben-Gurion's fears that the British might be dilatory, the withdrawal of their 100,000 troops was effective by May 1948. The UN's partition plan, which created an independent state of Israel, was approved by the General Assembly on 29 November 1947, with 33 members voting for the proposal, 13 opposing it and 10 abstaining. Jordan and Egypt occupied those territories of the former British Mandate in Palestine which had been assigned by the UN plan to a Palestinian Arab state, an entity which therefore did not come into being. Over

DAVID BEN-GURION (1886–1973)

1906 Emigrates to Palestine, then part of the Ottoman empire, from Plonsk, Poland, then ruled as part of tsarist Russia.

1912 Studies law at Istanbul University.

1915 Expelled from Palestine by Ottoman Turkish authorities on account of his political activities and moves to New York City.

1918 Joins British army as part of 38th Battalion, Jewish Legion; returns to Palestine after First World War.

1920 Assists in formation of Palestine's Zionist Labour Federation, subsequently becoming its general secretary.

1930 Mapai, precursor of Israel's later Labour Party, is formed under Ben-Gurion's leadership.

1935–48 Chairman of executive committee of the Jewish Agency for Palestine.

1948 Becomes Israel's first prime minister (serves 1948–53, 1955–63).

half of the indigenous Palestinian population in Israel's new national territory either fled or were expelled, and the state defended its borders successfully during the Arab–Israeli war of 1948–9.

'Our movement', as Ben-Gurion calls it, was Zionism and its aspiration became a reality when the 'destined Jewish state' was proclaimed on 14 May 1948. The reference to 'the last eighteen hundred years' underlines the claim to legitimacy. Repressive measures were imposed by the Roman imperial authorities in Judaea following the second major Jewish rebellion (AD 132–5) against their rule in the province. The Jews were expelled from Jerusalem and, in an attempt at erasing the region's Jewish identity, the Romans renamed Judaea 'Syria Palaestina'. Centuries of Jewish diaspora (dispersal) across the world followed. But Ben-Gurion's idealistic claim to Israeli modernity also matters. He suggests that the Arab masses will wish to emulate his people's literacy and prosperity, and that this will emancipate them from their leaders' hostility to Israel. Subsequent history would test this optimism.

Politics, predominantly, abhor a vacuum. If we do not fill it, others will. Let us, once and for all, slough the fancy that others may run our errand, as Britain promised 27 years ago. The polemics which agitated our movement this last decade – the 'to be or not to be' of the Mandate – are meaningless now.

Now final judgement is passed by the United Nations and the Mandatory. The Mandate is to end. There is neither prospect nor proposal that Britain be replaced as Mandatory by another power. There is one vivid conclusion we must draw – if governance has to be in Palestine, for the sake of the immigration and settlement which are unthinkable in a void, it will be our very own, or not at all.

'Perhaps we are unready, immature – but events will not wait on us'

It is hard to guess when the British will actually leave – three months, three years, or thirty, there is no telling. We know of 'provisional' occupations that lasted sixty. So let us be neither over-sanguine nor cast down. We are vitally concerned that Britain should not keep on implementing the policy of the white paper. What we want is mass immigration. There is an account to settle with Britain for shutting out thousands of Jews since the white paper appeared, and we may let history make that settlement. But a new chapter is opening – the instant chapter of what is to befall in immigration now.

No more protests and clamour, not another day of a vacuum in theory, jurisdiction and ethics. We shall bear the grave responsibility ourselves, untried though we have been in the arts and burdens of sovereignty for the last eighteen hundred years. The strain will be terrific. Between acquiescing in the white paper, with its locked gates and racial discrimination, and the assumption of sovereign power, there can, in truth, only be one choice. Perhaps we are unready, immature – but events will not wait on us. The international calendar will not synchronize itself to ours. We are set the problem and must solve it . . . supervised by the United Nations, helped by the United Nations, but in our own name, answerable to ourselves, with our own resources.

'As Jews, and more so as Zionists, we must forego facile optimism and barren despondency'

To establish a Jewish government will not be enough. Defence incalculably stronger and more up to date than anything improvised in the past 70 years . . . even that will not be enough. The British episode was important, but transient: intrinsically, and from the outset, short-lived. But we cannot look upon our dealings with the Arabs in that way.

This is our native land; it is not as birds of passage that we return to it. But it is situated in an area engulfed by Arabic-speaking peoples, mainly followers of Islam. Now, if ever, we must do more than make peace with them; we must achieve collaboration and alliance on equal terms. Remembering what Arab delegations from Palestine and its neighbours say in the General Assembly and in other places, talk of Arab–Jewish amity sounds fantastic, for the Arabs do not wish it. This is the attitude officially proclaimed, and it is not to be scoffed at. Neither should we overrate it, or be panicked by it. As Jews, and more so as Zionists, we must forego facile optimism and barren despondency. Basic facts are our allies: the tragedy of the Jews, the desolation of the Land, our unbreakable bond with it, our creativity – they have brought us thus far.

There are basic facts in the Arab realm also . . . and understanding of them should blow away our pessimism. They are the historical needs of the Arabs and of their states. A people's needs are not always articulate . . . but they cannot be stifled for long, eventually they force their swelling way into expression and satisfaction.

'The tragedy of the Jews, the desolation of the Land, our unbreakable bond with it, our creativity – they have brought us thus far'

History has been harsh to us, perhaps, setting burdensome conditions which complicate our homecoming, but it has set conditions too which . . . will not only allow but will compel Arab and Jew to work together because they need and complement each other.

Just two examples. Egypt is the biggest country in the Arab world. More than three-quarters of its population are *fellahin* [peasants] with an average monthly income of a pound sterling; nine-tenths of the fellahin are disease-ridden, all but five per cent illiterate. You cannot go on forever feeding this people on anti-Jewish incitement.

Iraq is thrice as large as Britain . . . after 25 years of independence, 85 per cent of the population are illiterate, half are infected and there is one doctor for every 8500 persons. And this is among the richest countries in the world. An anti-Jewish diet will not do indefinitely in Iraq either. I will not discuss ostensibly independent Transjordan, its poverty and neglect, many of us have visited it and know.

> *'If they do not learn from us and labour with us,*
> *it is with strangers, potent and tyrannous,*
> *that they will find themselves partnered'*

From our work in Palestine, from the society we are constructing, our economy and science, our culture and humanity, our social and fiscal order, and from no other source, must enlightenment come to our neighbours. If they do not learn from us and labour with us, it is with strangers, potent and tyrannous, that they will find themselves partnered.

They in turn have much to give us, they are blessed with what we lack. Great territories, ample for themselves and their children's children. We do not covet their expanses nor will we penetrate them – for we shall fight to end Diaspora in Arab lands as fiercely as we fought to end it in Europe, we want to be assembled wholly in our own Land. But if this region is to expand to the full, there must be reciprocity, there can be mutual aid – economic, political and cultural – between Jew and Arab. That is the necessity which will prevail, and the daily fulminations of their leaders should not alarm us unduly – they do not echo the real interests of the Arab peoples.

> *'There must be reciprocity, there can be mutual aid –*
> *economic, political and cultural –*
> *between Jew and Arab'*

It is now, here and now, from Jerusalem itself, that a call must go out to the Arab nations to join forces with Jewry and the destined Jewish state, and work shoulder to shoulder for our common good, for the peace and progress of sovereign equals.

'*The basic problem confronting the world today . . . is the preservation of human freedom*'

Eleanor Roosevelt

(1884–1962)

AMERICA'S FORMER FIRST LADY ADDRESSES THE UN GENERAL ASSEMBLY, PARIS, 9 DECEMBER 1948

The Universal Declaration of Human Rights was formally adopted by the United Nations General Assembly, meeting in Paris, on the day after Eleanor Roosevelt delivered this speech. It built on Western political thought's long tradition of defining constitutional rights and defending them against the encroachment of executive power – most notably so in England's Bill of Rights (1689) and the US Declaration of Independence (1776). The Declaration of the Rights of Man and of the Citizen, adopted by the French National Assembly in 1789, marked a further stage by universalizing the notions of human equality and freedom. The UN document, however, was a radical development since it included economic, social and cultural rights, as well as those civil and political liberties which had been the focus of previous definitions. The rights to form and join a trade union, to social security and to equal pay were now recognized alongside such traditional goals as freedom of assembly and equality before the law.

Like the UN itself, the Declaration's preoccupations were shaped by the recent world war as well as by the continuing threat of totalitarianism. Roosevelt's lively attack on the abuse of language by Soviet communism signified a general awareness of totalitarianism's deliberate obfuscation of words – a technique which George Orwell's novel *Nineteen Eighty-Four* (1949) would term 'Newspeak'. The USSR was among the eight abstentions when the Assembly voted on the Declaration.

Eleanor Roosevelt's upbringing, like that of her distant cousin and husband, Franklin Delano Roosevelt, was one of patrician privilege, and this speech was delivered in the distinctive accent she acquired at a finishing school in England. The paralysis of FDR's legs

ELEANOR ROOSEVELT (1884–1962)

1899–1902 Allenswood Academy, England.

1905 Marries Franklin Delano Roosevelt ('FDR').

1928 FDR (Democrat) elected governor of New York.

1932 FDR wins presidential election; re-elected 1936, 1940 and 1944.

1933–45 US first lady.

1941 Co-founder of Freedom House, an organization advocating international democratic freedoms and human rights.

1943 Founds the UN Association of the US, which lobbies for the UN's formation.

April 1945 President Roosevelt dies.

Jan 1946 First meeting of UN General Assembly in London.

1946–52 Serves as US delegate to UN General Assembly.

1961–2 Chair of Presidential Commission on Status of Women.

after contracting a high fever in 1921 meant that she had to be an unusually prominent first lady, frequently standing in for the president on public occasions and supporting with characteristic eloquence her particular causes of civil rights for African-Americans and relief for the unemployed who were the Great Depression's chief casualties. By this stage, however, she was already a veteran activist and, possibly impelled by the discovery in 1918 of FDR's long-term affair with her social secretary, she had thrown herself into the work of the Women's Trade Union League, which campaigned for its members' rights in the workplace. National admiration for her candour, energy and seriousness led President Truman to nominate her a delegate to the UN General Assembly, where, as chair of its Commission on Human Rights, she played a major role in drafting the Declaration. Roosevelt herself expressed the hope that this non-binding statement of customary law would become an 'international Magna Carta' and the Declaration's regular invocation by nation states has helped it fulfil that role. In 1988 the Council of Europe moved to apply its own document, the European Convention on Human Rights (1950), by establishing a Court of Human Rights. Forty-seven states scattered across the continent and adhering to the Council of Europe would give legal depth to the nobility of Eleanor Roosevelt's work.

We must not be confused about what freedom is. Basic human rights are simple and easily understood: freedom of speech and a free press; freedom of religion and worship; freedom of assembly and the right of petition; the right of men to be secure in their homes and free from unreasonable search and seizure and from arbitrary arrest and punishment . . .

Democracy, freedom, human rights have come to have a definite meaning to the people of the world which we must not allow any nation to so change that they are made synonymous with suppression and dictatorship. There are basic differences that show up even in the use of words between a democratic and a totalitarian country . . .

'Certain rights can never be granted to the government, but must be kept in the hands of the people'

The USSR representatives assert that they already have achieved many things which we, in what they call the 'bourgeois democracies', cannot achieve . . . Our government seems powerless to them because, in the last analysis, it is controlled by the people . . . they would say that the people of the USSR control their government by allowing [it] to have certain absolute rights. We, on the other hand, feel that certain rights can never be granted to the government, but must be kept in the hands of the people . . .

In the totalitarian state a trade union is an instrument used by the government to enforce duties, not to assert rights . . . Our trades unions, on the other hand, are solely the instrument of the workers themselves . . .

The right to work in the Soviet Union means the assignment of workers to do whatever task is given to them by the government . . . A society in which everyone works is not necessarily a free society and may indeed be a slave society; on the other hand, a society in which there is widespread economic insecurity can turn freedom into a barren and vapid right . . .

We in the United States have come to realize . . . that people have a right to demand that their government will not allow them to starve because . . . they cannot find work of the kind they are accustomed to doing . . . But we would not consider . . . that we had gained any freedom if we were compelled to follow a dictatorial assignment to work where and when we were told . . .

'A society in which everyone works is not necessarily a free society and may indeed be a slave society'

The basic problem confronting the world today . . . is the preservation of human freedom for the individual and consequently for the society of which he is a part. We are fighting this battle again today as it was fought at the time of the French Revolution and . . . of the American Revolution . . .

Freedom for our peoples is not only a right, but also a tool. Freedom of speech, freedom of the press, freedom of information, freedom of assembly – these are not just abstract ideals to us; they are tools with which we create . . . a way of life in which we can enjoy freedom . . . Basic decisions of our society are made through the expressed will of the people. That is why when we see these liberties threatened, instead of falling apart, our nation becomes unified and our democracies come together . . . in spite of our varied backgrounds and many racial strains.

'Basic decisions of our society are made through the expressed will of the people'

In the United States we have a capitalist economy. That is because public opinion favours that type of economy under the conditions in which we live. But we have imposed certain restraints; for instance, we have anti-trust laws. These are the legal evidence of the determination of the American people to maintain an economy of free competition and not to allow monopolies to take away the people's freedom . . .

'The basic problem confronting the world today . . .
is the preservation of human freedom.'

The USSR claims it has reached a point where all races within her borders are officially considered equal . . . and they insist that they have no discrimination where minorities are considered. This is a laudable objective but there are other aspects of the development of freedom . . . which are essential before the mere absence of discrimination is worth much . . . It is these other freedoms – the basic freedoms of speech, of the press, of religion and conscience, of assembly, of fair trial and freedom from arbitrary arrest and punishment – which a totalitarian government cannot safely give to its people and which give meaning to freedom from discrimination . . .

Among free men the end cannot justify the means. We know the patterns of totalitarianism – the single political party, the control of schools, press, radio, the arts, the sciences and the church to support autocratic authority; these are the age-old patterns against which men have struggled for three thousand years. These are the signs of reaction, retreat and retrogression . . .

The field of human rights is not one in which compromise on fundamental principles is possible . . . The future must see the broadening of human rights throughout the world. People who have glimpsed freedom will never be content until they have secured it for themselves. In a truest sense, human rights are a fundamental object of law and government in a just society. Human rights exist to the degree that they are respected by people in relations with each other and by governments in relations with their citizens . . .

'I pray Almighty God that we may win another victory here for the rights and freedoms of all men'

The propaganda we have witnessed in the recent past, like that we perceive in these days, seeks to impugn, to undermine and to destroy the liberty and independence of peoples. Such propaganda poses to all peoples the issue whether to doubt their heritage of rights . . . or to accept the challenge . . . and stand steadfast in the struggle to maintain and enlarge human freedoms . . . The immediate test is not only . . . the extent to which human rights and freedoms have already been achieved, but the direction in which the world is moving . . .

The place to discuss the issue of human rights is in the forum of the United Nations . . . where we can consider together our mutual problems and take advantage of our differences in experience. It is inherent in our firm attachment to democracy and freedom that we stand always ready to use the fundamental democratic procedures of honest discussion and negotiation . . . I pray Almighty God that we may win another victory here for the rights and freedoms of all men.

its tug at the heart strings. But it is the speech's substance which impresses with its superb account of the Far East's impact on America's destiny and its evaluation of the country's stature as a great Pacific power. The geopolitical details are brought to life with immense flair and an acute strategic sense, and subsequent 20th-century history would show the US's role in the Pacific Rim supplementing her status as an Atlantic power.

By 1951 MacArthur had been away from the US for 11 years, but even before then the circumstances of high command had encouraged his independence of mind. When the Commonwealth of the Philippines attained semi-autonomy from the US in 1935, he had supervised the subsequent creation of the country's national army. MacArthur was Japan's effective ruler in the immediate postwar period and the country's constitution, effective from 1947 onwards, was drafted by his staff. The sight of a general exercising civilian power encouraged comparisons with the shoguns of Japan's past. But the man who stood before Congress, though imperious, was visibly no autocrat. It was rather the unique range of his experiences and responsibilities which lent authority to MacArthur's insights and earned him the plaudits of the people's representatives.

I address you with neither rancour nor bitterness in the fading twilight of life. The issues are global and so interlocked that to consider the problems of one sector, oblivious to those of another, is but to court disaster for the whole.

While Asia is commonly referred to as the Gateway to Europe, it is no less true that Europe is the Gateway to Asia, and the broad influence of the one cannot fail to have its impact upon the other. The communist threat is a global one. You cannot appease or otherwise surrender to communism in Asia without simultaneously undermining our efforts to halt its advance in Europe.

'The communist threat is a global one'

The peoples of Asia found their opportunity in the war just past to throw off the shackles of colonialism and now see the dawn of new opportunity, a heretofore unfelt dignity, and the self-respect of political freedom. Mustering half the world's population and 60 per cent of its natural resources, these peoples are rapidly consolidating a new force, both moral and material. This is the direction of Asian progress and it may not be stopped. It is a corollary to the shift of the world economic frontiers as the whole epicentre of world affairs rotates back towards the area whence it started.

The Asian peoples covet the right to shape their own free destiny. What they seek now is the dignity of equality and not the shame of subjugation. These political–social conditions . . . form a backdrop to contemporary planning which must be thoughtfully considered if we are to avoid the pitfalls of unrealism.

Of more direct . . . bearing upon our national security are the changes wrought in the strategic potential of the Pacific Ocean in the course of the past war. Prior thereto the western strategic frontier of the United States lay on the littoral line of the Americas. The Pacific was a potential area of advance for any predatory force intent upon striking at the bordering land areas.

All this was changed by our Pacific victory. Our strategic frontier then shifted to embrace the entire Pacific Ocean, which became a vast moat to protect us as long as we held it. We control it to the shores of Asia by a chain of islands extending in an arc from the Aleutians to the Marianas held by us and our free allies. From this island chain we can dominate with sea and air power every Asiatic port from Vladivostok to Singapore.

The holding of this littoral defence line in the western Pacific is entirely dependent upon holding all segments thereof. For that reason, I have strongly recommended . . . that under no circumstances must Formosa fall under communist control. Such an eventuality . . . might well force our western frontier back to the coast of California, Oregon and Washington.

'The Asian peoples covet the right to shape their own free destiny'

China, up to 50 years ago, was compartmented into groups divided against each other. At the turn of the century . . . efforts towards greater homogeneity produced the start of a nationalist urge. This . . . has been brought to its greatest fruition under the present regime. Through these past 50 years the Chinese people have thus become militarized in their concepts and in their ideals . . . with a lust for expansion and increased power.

The Japanese people, since the war, have undergone the greatest reformation recorded in modern history. Politically, economically and socially, Japan is now abreast of many free nations. I know of no nation more serene, orderly and industrious.

Of our former ward, the Philippines, we can look forward in confidence that . . . a healthy nation will grow. In our hour of need they did not fail us. The Philippines stand as a mighty bulwark of Christianity in the Far East, and its capacity for high moral leadership in Asia is unlimited.

I now turn to the Korean conflict. Our victory was complete, and our objectives within reach, when Red China intervened. This created a new war and . . . a situation which called for new decisions in the diplomatic sphere to permit the realistic adjustment of military strategy. Such decisions have not been forthcoming.

I felt that military necessity in the conduct of the war made necessary: first, the intensification of our economic blockade against China; two, the imposition of a naval blockade against the China coast; three, removal of restrictions on air reconnaissance of China's coastal areas; four, removal of restrictions on the forces of the Republic of China on Formosa . . .

We could hold in Korea by constant manoeuvre . . . but we could hope at best for only an indecisive campaign . . . if the enemy utilized its full military potential.

'The Japanese people, since the war, have undergone the greatest reformation recorded in modern history'

It has been said, in effect, that I was a warmonger. Nothing could be further from the truth. I know war as few other men now living know it, and nothing to me is more revolting. I have long advocated its complete abolition, as its very destructiveness on both friend and foe has rendered it useless as a means of settling international disputes. But once war is forced upon us, there is no other alternative than . . . to bring it to a swift end. War's every object is victory, not prolonged indecision.

The tragedy of Korea is further heightened by the fact that its military action is confined to its territorial limits. It condemns that nation . . . to suffer the devastating impact of full naval and air bombardment while the enemy's sanctuaries are fully protected from such attack.

The magnificence of the courage and fortitude of the Korean people defies description. They have chosen death rather than slavery. Their last words to me were: 'Don't scuttle the Pacific!'

'War's every object is victory, not prolonged indecision'

I am closing my 52 years of military service. When I joined the army . . . it was the fulfilment of all my boyish hopes and dreams. The world has turned over many times since I took the oath on the plain at West Point, and the hopes and dreams have long since vanished, but I still remember the refrain of one of the most popular barrack ballads of that day which proclaimed most proudly that 'old soldiers never die; they just fade away'.

And like the old soldier of that ballad, I now close my military career and just fade away, an old soldier who tried to do his duty as God gave him the light to see that duty.

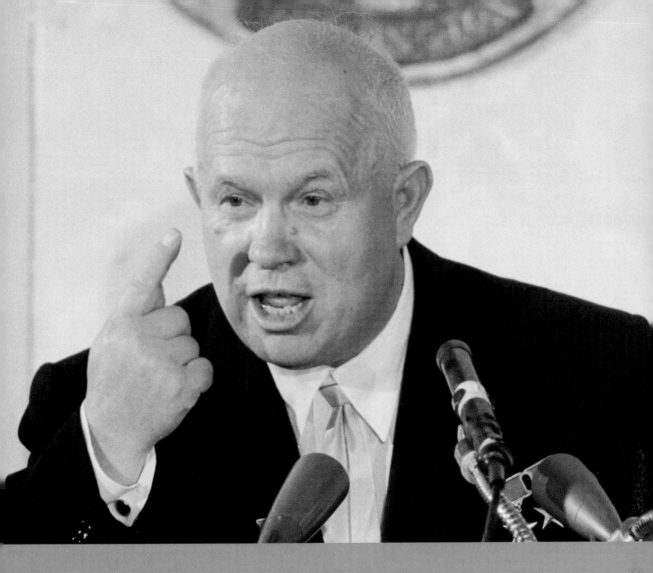

'The cult of the individual brought about rude violation of party democracy'

Nikita Khrushchev

(1894–1971)

THE SOVIET PRESIDENT DENOUNCES STALIN AT THE 20TH CONGRESS OF THE
SOVIET COMMUNIST PARTY, MOSCOW, 25 FEBRUARY 1956

The 20th Congress was the first one to be held after Stalin's death in 1953 and his successor, Nikita Khrushchev, was promoting liberalization. Greater freedom of information, foreign cultural links, the freeing of some eight million political prisoners: all constituted a 'Khrushchev thaw'. It took some four hours to deliver the entire speech and its content caused some delegates to suffer heart attacks. Others, similarly disabused, committed suicide afterwards. The idealized account of Lenin was tactically astute and intended to show that Stalin had betrayed the revolutionary legacy. The Congress was meeting in closed session when Khrushchev addressed it and the speech was sent to regional party secretaries who briefed party members on its contents. Emphasis on its secrecy contributed to the speech's celebrity and Khrushchev's aides ensured that copies were obtained by Western newspapers, whose publication of the text caused an international sensation.

The speech's background is one of rivalry within the Soviet leadership and Khrushchev was intent on consolidating his position. He had deposed Lavrenti Beria, the state security chief, who was executed in December 1953. Other rivals included Vyacheslav Molotov and Georgi Malenkov, both influential members of the Politburo (or Presidium), which administered the USSR's Communist Party and formulated its policies. These old-style Stalinists interpreted the speech, correctly, as a personal attack. The plot they proceeded to plan was exposed in May 1957 and Khrushchev subsequently expelled them from the party. Despite his attack on Stalinist methods of government, Khrushchev's speech did not criticize past economic policies – including the collectivization of agriculture which had caused the deaths of an officially estimated 12 million. The denunciation was cleverly selective for two

NIKITA KHRUSHCHEV (1894–1971)

1918 Joins Bolshevik Party.

1934 Appointed first secretary of the Moscow City Committee; impresses with work overseeing construction of the city's subway system.

1934 Elected to Central Committee of the Communist Party of the Soviet Union.

1938 Appointed first secretary of Ukrainian Central Committee.

1939 Becomes full member of the Politburo.

1941–5 Serves as a political commissar, with the rank of lieutenant general.

Sept 1953 Becomes first secretary of the Communist Party.

March 1958 Becomes chairman of the Council of Ministers of the USSR.

Oct 1964 Removed from office by the Soviet Presidium, a decision subsequently approved by the Communist Party's Central Committee.

reasons: the party's authority needed to be maintained, and Khrushchev was implicated in the Stalinist past – which is why his tirade struck many as hypocritical.

Fears that the thaw was getting out of hand came to a head in the autumn of 1956, when Hungary erupted in anti-communist rebellion and the premier Imre Nagy abolished the single-party system. The Presidium reacted by sending in Soviet troops to re-establish Hungarian communist control. In October workers rioted in the Polish city of Poznan, and the government there had to introduce liberalizing measures in order to survive. These insurgencies seemed to be a direct consequence of hopes aroused by Khrushchev's speech and therefore provided ammunition for his critics. He continued nonetheless with his critique of the past and a symbolic dénouement arrived in 1961, when Stalin's body was removed from public view and buried outside the Kremlin wall.

Having embraced 'peaceful coexistence' with the West, Khrushchev's position was then undermined by the Cuban Missile Crisis of October 1962. He had to agree to the US demand that the Soviets remove the weapons they had sent to Cuba, and the loss of face was the prelude to his ejection from office. There was, however, an important Khrushchev legacy. His speech influenced many younger communist officials, including Mikhail Gorbachev, whose aspirations as general secretary (1985–91) often mirrored those of Khrushchev.

After Stalin's death the central committee began explaining that it is foreign to the spirit of Marxism–Leninism to elevate one person, to transform him into a superman. Such a belief about a man, and specifically about Stalin, was cultivated among us for many years.

At present we are concerned with how the cult of Stalin became the source of a whole series of exceedingly serious perversions of party principles, of party democracy, of revolutionary legality.

'The cult of Stalin became the source of a whole series of exceedingly serious perversions of party principles'

The great modesty of the genius of the revolution, Vladimir Ilyich Lenin, is known. Lenin always stressed the role of the people as the creator of history. Lenin mercilessly stigmatized every manifestation of the cult of the individual. He patiently explained his opinions to others.

Lenin detected in Stalin those negative characteristics which resulted later in grave consequences. Fearing the future fate of the Soviet nation, Lenin pointed out that it was necessary to consider transferring Stalin from the position of general secretary because

Stalin did not have a proper attitude towards his comrades. As later events have proven, Lenin's anxiety was justified.

Stalin, who absolutely did not tolerate collegiality in leadership and in work, acted not through persuasion, but by imposing his concepts. Stalin originated the concept 'enemy of the people'. This term made possible the use of the cruellest repression against anyone who disagreed with Stalin, against those who were only suspected of hostile intent. 'Confessions' were acquired through physical pressures. Innocent individuals became victims. Mass arrests and deportations of many thousands of people, execution without trial, created conditions of insecurity, fear and even desperation.

Vladimir Ilyich demanded uncompromising dealings with the enemies of the revolution. Lenin used such methods, however, only against actual class enemies and not against those who blunder. Stalin, on the other hand, used extreme methods and mass repressions at a time when the revolution was already victorious.

'Stalin trampled on the principle of collective party leadership'

Lenin considered it absolutely necessary that the party discuss at length all questions bearing on the development of government. After Lenin's death, Stalin trampled on the principle of collective party leadership. Of the 139 members and candidates of the central committee who were elected at the 17th Congress, 98 persons, 70 per cent, were arrested and shot. It is inconceivable that a congress so composed could have elected a central committee in which a majority would prove to be enemies of the party. Delegates were active participants in the building of our socialist state; many of them suffered and fought during the pre-revolutionary years; they fought their enemies valiantly and often looked into the face of death. How, then, can we believe that such people had joined the camps of the enemies of socialism?

Lenin taught that the application of revolutionary violence is necessitated by the resistance of the exploiting classes, and this referred to the era when the exploiting classes existed and were powerful. As soon as the nation's political situation had improved, Lenin gave instructions to stop mass terror and to abolish the death penalty. Stalin deviated from these precepts. Terror was actually directed against the honest workers of the party; lying, slanderous and absurd accusations were made against them.

Stalin was a very distrustful man. He could look at a man and say: 'Why are your eyes so shifty today?' The sickly suspicion created in him a general distrust. Everywhere and in everything he saw 'enemies', 'two-facers' and 'spies'.

The power accumulated in the hands of one person, Stalin, led to serious consequences during the great patriotic war. When we look at many of our novels, films and historical–scientific studies, the role of Stalin in the patriotic war appears to be entirely improbable. Stalin had foreseen everything. The epic victory is ascribed as being completely due to the strategic genius of Stalin.

Stalin advanced the thesis that our nation experienced an 'unexpected' attack by the Germans. But, comrades, this is completely untrue. As soon as Hitler came to power, he assigned to himself the task of liquidating communism. The fascists were saying this openly. Despite grave warnings, the necessary steps were not taken to prepare. We paid with great losses – until our generals succeeded in altering the situation. Stalin tried to inculcate the notion that the victories gained by the Soviet nation were all due to the genius of Stalin and of no one else. Let us take our military films. They make us feel sick. Let us recall *The Fall of Berlin*. Here only Stalin acts. He does not reckon with anyone. He asks no one for advice. Everything is shown to the people in this false light. Not Stalin, but the party as a whole, the Soviet government, our heroic army, its talented leaders and brave soldiers, the whole Soviet nation – these are the ones who assured victory in the great patriotic war.

Comrades! The cult of the individual brought about rude violation of party democracy, sterile administration, deviations, cover-ups of shortcomings, and varnishings of reality.

Why did not members of the politburo assert themselves in time? Initially, many backed Stalin because he was one of the strongest Marxists and his logic, his strength and his will greatly influenced party work. After Lenin's death Stalin actively fought against those who deviated from the correct Leninist path. This fight was indispensable. Later, however, Stalin began to fight honest Soviet people.

'Everywhere and in everything he saw "enemies", "two-facers" and "spies"'

Comrades! Lenin had often stressed that modesty is an absolutely integral part of a real Bolshevik. We cannot say that we have been following this Leninist example in all respects. We must correct this. But this should be done calmly. We cannot let this matter get out of the party, especially not to the press.

Comrades! We must abolish the cult of the individual once and for all.

The fact that we present in all their ramifications the basic problems of overcoming the cult of the individual is evidence of the great moral and political strength of our party. We are absolutely certain that our party, armed with the historical resolutions of the 20th Congress, will lead the Soviet people to new successes.

Long live the victorious banner of our party – Leninism!

'The government resorted to epic weapons for squalid and trivial ends'

Aneurin Bevan

(1897–1960)

THE SHADOW FOREIGN SECRETARY ATTACKS THE GOVERNMENT'S POLICY IN
THE MIDDLE EAST; HOUSE OF COMMONS, LONDON, 5 DECEMBER 1956

'The government resorted to epic weapons for squalid and trivial ends'

On 26 July 1956 President Gamal Abdel Nasser of Egypt announced that his government would nationalize the Suez Canal Company which operated the waterway linking Port Said on the Mediterranean with Suez on the Red Sea. Britain and France, the company's shareholders, reacted by colluding with Israel and encouraging it to invade Egypt. A Franco-British force could then intervene, using as a pretext the need to separate the combatants. Forcing the Israeli and Egyptian armies apart on either side of the canal, the French and British could then resume control of its management. The US was not informed of these plans.

British radicals had always decried secret diplomacy, and Aneurin Bevan's combination of verbal mischief with oratorical passion had made him the star of the Labour Party's left-wing faction. His speech teases out inconsistencies in the government's public position, contradictions which resulted from its dishonesty about the campaign's motives. The mockery had a steely edge. Bevan, helped by the slight stutter he used to dramatic effect, was inveighing against the reactionary attitudes he regarded as an imbecilic brake on human progress.

The canal had played an important British strategic role as a communications link with the country's Asian colonies, and it had recently assumed a novel economic significance as a conduit for oil tankers. By July 1956 the last British troops guarding the canal had been withdrawn following Nasser's repudiation five years earlier of the Anglo-Egyptian Treaty (1936), which had confirmed the canal's status as a neutral zone under British protection. Charges to be levied on canal traffic were now earmarked by Nasser to help finance the Aswan Dam's construction. Britain and the US had withdrawn an earlier offer to meet the scheme's costs.

ANEURIN BEVAN (1897–1960)

1929 Elected member of Parliament (Labour) for Ebbw Vale, South Wales.

1945–51 Minister of health in Britain's Labour government; oversees introduction (1948) of the National Health Service.

1951 Minister of labour, but resigns over introduction of prescription charges for dental care and spectacles.

1951 Labour is voted out of office in the general election; Bevan initiates a left–right split within his party and leads opposition to high defence expenditure.

1955 Defeated in contest for leadership of the Labour Party.

1956–9 Shadow foreign secretary.

1957 Rejects unilateral nuclear disarmament in a speech to the Labour Party conference.

Canal nationalization was also a way of promoting Nasser as a hero of 'the Arab world'. The anti-colonial spirit he represented was a popular Egyptian sentiment, especially since Britain's influence on the country's government and army had survived Egypt's formal independence from the British in 1922 and lasted until the 1952 coup which brought Nasser to power. He also discomfited France with his profound influence on Arab nationalists in its north African colonies.

Initially, the plan worked. Israel invaded the Sinai on 29 October 1956. Franco-British forces stormed northwestern Sinai's beaches on 5 and 6 November. Port Said suffered heavy damage. The canal area was seized. But the US demanded an immediate ceasefire. In early November it was condemning the Soviet invasion which suppressed Hungary's national rebellion. Consistency, and irritation, dictated US opposition to the Suez expedition as another instance of a country's sovereign territory being invaded. Eisenhower threatened to sell the US treasury's sterling assets and thereby cause a run on the pound unless Britain withdrew. The Franco-British force left Egypt within weeks and Anthony Eden resigned as prime minister on 10 January 1957.

Bevan's speech marks Britain's enforced recognition of the limits to her power. Postcolonial realism, however, had unexpected consequences. Within a year Bevan was arguing that Britain needed its own nuclear deterrent – a policy reversal which dismayed erstwhile 'Bevanites'.

' I have been looking through the various objectives and reasons that the government have given to the House of Commons for making war on Egypt, and it really is desirable that when a nation makes war upon another nation, it should be quite clear why it does so. There is, in fact, no correspondence whatsoever between the reasons given today and the reasons set out by the prime minister at the beginning.

On 30 October, the prime minister said that the purpose was, first, 'to seek to separate the combatants'; second, 'to remove the risk to free passage through the canal'. The speech we have heard today is the first speech in which that subject has been dropped . . . The right honourable and learned gentleman . . . has said that when we landed in Port Said there was already every reason to believe that both Egypt and Israel had agreed to a ceasefire.

'Our ambitions soar the further away we are from realizing them'

We are telling the nation and the world that having decided upon the course, we went on with it despite the fact that the objective we had set ourselves had already been achieved, namely, the separation of the combatants. As to the objective of removing the risk to free passage through the canal, I must confess that I have been astonished at this also. We sent an

'The government resorted to epic weapons for squalid and trivial ends'

ultimatum to Egypt by which we told her that unless she agreed to our landing in Ismailia, Suez and Port Said, we should make war upon her. Did we really believe that Nasser was going to give in at once? He did what anybody would have thought he would do. He sank ships in the canal, the wicked man. The result is that the first objective realized was the opposite of the one we set out to achieve; the canal was blocked, and it is still blocked.

On 1 November, we were told the reason was 'to stop hostilities' and 'prevent a resumption of them'. But hostilities had already been practically stopped. On 3 November, our objectives became much more ambitious – 'to deal with all the outstanding problems in the Middle East' . . .

Our ambitions soar the further away we are from realizing them. After having insulted the United States, . . . after having driven the whole of the Arab world into one solid phalanx behind Nasser, we were then going to deal with all the outstanding problems in the Middle East.

'We cannot run the processes of modern society by attempting to impose our will upon nations by armed force'

The next objective of which we were told was to ensure that the Israeli forces withdrew from Egyptian territory. That is a remarkable war aim, is it not? To establish our case before the eyes of the world, Israel being the wicked invader, we being the nice friend of Egypt, went to protect her from the Israelis, but, unfortunately, we had to bomb the Egyptians first . . .

We started this operation in order to give Nasser a black eye – if we could, to overthrow him – but, in any case, to secure control of the canal . . .

In fact, very few of the activities at the beginning of October are credible except upon the assumption that the French and British governments knew that something was going to happen in Egypt . . .

These were objectives . . . that were not realizable by the means that we adopted. These civil, social and political objectives in modern society are not attainable by armed force. It is clear . . . that there is such bitter feeling against Western imperialism . . . among millions of people that they are not prepared to keep the arteries of European commerce alive and intact if they themselves want to cut them.

We cannot run the processes of modern society by attempting to impose our will upon nations by armed force. Therefore . . . whatever may have been the morality of the world outlook and acquire the proletarian, communist world outlook so that they can fully fit in with the needs of the new society . . .

Among students and intellectuals there has recently been a falling-off in ideological and political work . . . It seems as if Marxism, once all the rage, is currently not so much in fashion. To counter these tendencies, we must strengthen our ideological and political work . . . Not to have a correct political orientation is like not having a soul.

Letting a hundred flowers blossom and a hundred schools of thought contend is the policy for promoting progress in the arts and sciences and a flourishing socialist culture in our land. Different forms and styles in art should develop freely and different schools in science should contend freely. We think that it is harmful . . . if administrative measures are used to impose one particular style of art or school of thought and to ban another.

Questions of right and wrong in the arts and science should be settled through free discussion . . . and through practical work in these fields. They should not be settled in an over-simple manner. A period of trial is often needed to determine whether something is right or wrong.

Throughout history at the outset new and correct things often failed to win recognition from the majority of people and had to develop by twists and turns through struggle. Often, correct and good things were first regarded not as fragrant flowers but as poisonous weeds. Copernicus's theory of the solar system and Darwin's theory of evolution were once dismissed as erroneous and had to win out over bitter opposition . . .

'Often, correct and good things were first regarded not as fragrant flowers but as poisonous weeds'

In a socialist society, the conditions for the growth of the new are . . . far superior to those in the old society. Nevertheless, it often happens that new, rising forces are held back and sound ideas stifled. Besides even in the absence of their deliberate suppression, the growth of new things may be hindered simply through lack of discernment. It is therefore necessary . . . to encourage free discussion and avoid hasty conclusions.

Marxism, too, has developed through struggle . . . In China the remoulding of the petty bourgeoisie has only just started. Class struggle is by no means over. The proletariat seeks to transform the world according to its own world outlook, and so does the bourgeoisie . . . the question of which will win out, socialism or capitalism, is not really settled yet . . . Therefore Marxism must continue to develop through struggle . . . What is correct inevitably develops in the course of struggle with what is wrong. The true, the

*'Let a hundred flowers blossom. Let a hundred schools
of thought contend'*

good and the beautiful always exist by contrast with the false, the evil and the ugly, and grow in struggle with them. As soon as something erroneous is rejected and a particular truth accepted by mankind, new truths begin to struggle with new errors. Such struggles will never end. This is the law of development of truth and, naturally, of Marxism.

'The question of which will win out, socialism or capitalism, is not really settled yet'

It will take a fairly long period of time to decide the issue in the ideological struggle between socialism and capitalism in our country . . . Ideological struggle differs from other forms of struggle, since the only method used is painstaking reasoning, and not crude coercion . . . Although there are defects and mistakes in our work, every fair-minded person can see . . . that we have already achieved great success and will achieve still greater ones. The vast majority of the bourgeoisie and the intellectuals who come from the old society are patriotic . . . they know they will have nothing to fall back on and their future cannot possibly be bright if they turn away from the socialist cause and from the working people led by the Communist Party . . .

Marxists should not be afraid of criticism from any quarter . . . Fighting against wrong ideas is like being vaccinated – a man develops greater immunity . . . Plants raised in hothouses are unlikely to be hardy. Carrying out the policy of letting a hundred flowers bloom and a hundred schools of thought contend will . . . strengthen the leading position of Marxism in the ideological field.

What should our policy be towards non-Marxist ideas? . . . Will it do to ban such ideas . . . ? Certainly not. It is not only futile but very harmful to use crude methods in dealing with . . . questions about man's mental world. You may ban the expression of wrong ideas, but the ideas will still be there . . . Therefore, it is only by employing the method of discussion, criticism and reasoning . . . that we can really settle issues . . . Mistakes must be criticized and poisonous weeds fought wherever they crop up. However, such criticism should not be dogmatic . . . we must carefully distinguish between what is really a poisonous weed and what is really a fragrant flower . . .

In their political activities, how should our people judge whether a person's words and deeds are right or wrong? . . . we consider that words and deeds should be beneficial to socialist transformation. They should help to strengthen . . . the leadership of the Communist Party. These political criteria are applicable to all activities in the arts and sciences. In a socialist country like ours, can there possibly be any useful or scientific or artistic activity which runs counter to these political criteria?

The senator from Massachusetts had consistently emphasized his comparative youth while campaigning to gain the Democrats' nomination to contest the 1960 US presidential election. Success in that election would confirm the appeal of his emphasis on novelty, freshness and vigour – themes which would therefore also typify JFK's speeches as president. Theodore (Ted) C. Sorensen was invariably by his side, first as senatorial assistant and then as special counsel to the president. Jack Kennedy had a literary side to him and in the young lawyer from Nebraska he found a staffer with a similar feel for language. The speeches they wrote together came to define a new era in American life, an era when the country was enjoined to turn its back on the immediate past of the 1950s as a time of 'drugged and fitful sleep'.

President Eisenhower, Kennedy's predecessor, had ended the war in Korea and warned against the development of a 'military–industrial complex' within US big business. But Kennedy campaigned for the presidency as a Cold War partisan, hence his reference here to the 'single-minded advance of the communist system'. A lazy American administration, he claimed, had allowed the Soviets to acquire a superiority in nuclear-armed missiles. There was a 'missile gap' and the US had to catch up. The campaign promise was more than fulfilled. By October 1962 the US had more than 25,000 nuclear weapons, while the USSR had less than half that number.

Kennedy was the first Catholic to be elected president, and the widespread American suspicion of his church as a foreign institution obliged him to assert his independence of the papacy's political influence. His own poor health was another drawback to the candidacy, and Kennedy's puffy expression was attributable to the steroids he took as treatment for Addison's disease, an endocrine disorder. A tan masked the sickness – and so

JOHN F. KENNEDY (1917–63)

June 1940 Graduates from Harvard University.

June 1944 Awarded Purple Heart for wartime bravery.

Nov 1952 Elected senator for Massachusetts (re-elected 1958).

July 1960 Wins Democratic presidential nomination.

Nov 1960 Narrowly defeats Richard Nixon to become 35th president of the USA.

Jan 1961 Inauguration as president.

April 1961 Bay of Pigs invasion of Cuba fails.

Oct 1962 Cuban Missile Crisis.

Aug 1963 Signs Partial Test Ban Treaty in Moscow.

22 Nov 1963 Assassinated in Dallas, Texas.

'We stand today on the edge of a New Frontier'

did the speeches. Those listening to a man committed to 'strong, creative . . . leadership' and to the provision of 'intellectual and moral strength' assumed that he was himself healthy.

California was a good place to explore the metaphor of a 'New Frontier' since it was the westward expansion of the US which had produced the 'pioneer spirit'. Subliminal imagery involving cowboys and stage-coaches was now enrolled to describe the 1960 frontier whose opportunities and perils were both intellectual and practical. Space had to be conquered and ignorance abolished, peace ought to be attained and poverty alleviated. Not all young men, however, were equally qualified to join the new pioneers, and Kennedy's patronizing reference to his Republican opponent, Richard Nixon, was calculated to wound. *Poor Richard's Almanack*, an annual publication written by Benjamin Franklin, enjoyed success in mid-18th-century America, with its collection of homely proverbs and traditional sayings appealing especially to the self-educated. Nonetheless, the oratory of this Harvard-educated politician also invoked the American tradition of self-help. FDR's New Deal had 'promised security and succour'. But JFK's New Frontier required the American people to supply their own frontier spirit. If the US was to endure as a democracy, its people had work to do.

'I hope that no American . . . will waste his franchise by voting either for me or against me solely on account of my religious affiliation. It is not relevant . . . I am telling you now what you are entitled to know: that my decisions on any public policy will be my own – as an American, a Democrat and a free man . . .

After eight years of drugged and fitful sleep, this nation needs strong, creative Democratic leadership in the White House . . . the American people expect more from us than cries of indignation and attack. The times are too grave, the challenge too urgent, and the stakes too high to permit the customary passions of political debate . . .

For the world is changing. The old era is ending. The old ways will not do.

There are new and more terrible weapons, new and uncertain nations, new pressures of population and deprivation. One-third of the world, it has been said, may be free, but one-third is the victim of cruel repression – and the other one-third is rocked by the pangs of poverty, hunger and envy. More energy is released by the awakening of these new nations than by the fission of the atom itself. For the world is changing.

Meanwhile, communist influence has penetrated further into Asia, stood astride the Middle East and now festers some 90 miles off the coast of Florida.

The world has been close to war before, but now man, who has survived all previous threats to his existence, has taken into his mortal hands the power to exterminate the entire species some seven times over.

'For the world is changing. The old era is ending. The old ways will not do'

Here at home, the changing face of the future is equally revolutionary . . .

An urban population explosion has overcrowded our schools, cluttered up our suburbs and increased the squalor of our slums.

A peaceful revolution for human rights, demanding an end to racial discrimination, has strained at the leashes imposed by timid executive leadership . . .

And a revolution of automation finds machines replacing men in the mines and mills of America, without replacing their incomes or their training . . .

There has also been a change – a slippage – in our intellectual and moral strength. Seven lean years of drought and famine have withered a field of ideas. Blight has descended . . . and a dry rot, beginning in Washington, is seeping into every corner of America – in the expense account way of life, the confusion between what is legal and what is right. Too many Americans have lost their way, their will and their sense of historic purpose.

It is a time, in short, for a new generation of leadership – new men to cope with new problems and new opportunities.

All over the world, particularly in the newer nations, young men are coming to power – men who are not bound by the traditions of the past, men who are not blinded by the old fears and hates and rivalries, young men who can cast off the old slogans and delusions and suspicions.

'It is a time, in short, for a new generation of leadership – new men to cope with new problems and new opportunities'

The Republican nominee-to-be, of course, is also a young man. But . . . his party is the party of the past. His speeches are generalities from *Poor Richard's Almanack* . . . Their pledge is a pledge to the status quo – and today there can be no status quo.

For I stand tonight facing west on what was once the last frontier. From the lands that stretch 3000 miles behind me, the pioneers of old gave up their safety, their comfort and sometimes their lives to build a new world here in the west. They were not the captives of their own doubts . . . Their motto was not 'every man for himself' but 'all for the common cause'. They were determined to make that new world strong and free, to overcome its hazards and its hardships, to conquer the enemies that threatened from without and within. Today some would say . . . that all the battles have been won – that there is no longer an American frontier. But . . . we stand today on the edge of a New Frontier – the frontier of the 1960s, a frontier of unknown opportunities and perils, a frontier of unfulfilled hopes and threats . . .

Franklin Roosevelt's New Deal promised security and succour to those in need. But the New Frontier of which I speak is not a set of promises – it is a set of challenges. It sums up not what I intend to offer the American people, but what I intend to ask of them . . .

But I tell you the New Frontier is here, whether we seek it or not. Beyond that frontier are the uncharted areas of science and space, unsolved problems of peace and war, unconquered pockets of ignorance and prejudice, unanswered questions of poverty and surplus . . .

But I believe the times demand new invention, innovation, imagination, decision. I am asking each of you to be pioneers on that New Frontier . . .

'The New Frontier of which I speak is not a set of promises – it is a set of challenges'

We must prove all over again whether this nation – or any nation so conceived – can long endure; whether our society – with its freedom of choice, its breadth of opportunity, its range of alternatives – can compare with the single-minded advance of the communist system.

Can a nation organized and governed such as ours endure? That is the real question. Have we the nerve and the will?

That is the question of the New Frontier. That is the choice our nation must make – a choice that lies not merely between two men or two parties, but between the public interest and private comfort; between national greatness and national decline; between the fresh air of progress and the stale, dank atmosphere of 'normalcy'; between determined dedication and creeping democracy.

All mankind waits upon our decision. A whole world looks to see what we will do. We cannot fail their trust, we cannot fail to try . . .

Recall with me the words of Isaiah: 'They that wait upon the Lord shall renew their strength; they shall mount up with wings as eagles; they shall run and not be weary.'

As we face the coming challenge, we too shall wait upon the Lord and ask that He renew our strength. Then shall we be equal to the test. Then we shall not be weary. And then we shall prevail.

'Ask not what your country can do for you; ask what you can do for your country'

John F. Kennedy

(1917–63)

THE 35TH PRESIDENT OF THE USA DELIVERS HIS INAUGURAL ADDRESS; WASHINGTON, 20 JANUARY 1961

*Ask not what your country can do for you;
ask what you can do for your country'*

Johnn F. Kennedy's inaugural address as president displayed both clarity of thought and concision of expression. Its celebrity was immediate and has proved to be lasting. That this should be so owes much to the fact that the speech is a classically fine example of English prose at its unadorned best. The vocabulary is simple, the sentence construction is well balanced, relative clauses are kept under control. Similes and metaphors do not, on the whole, overreach themselves. The excessively elaborate 'beachhead of cooperation' and 'jungle of suspicion' contrast with the elegant lucidity which is this speech's predominant tone. Kennedy knew what he wanted to say and how to say it.

'New Frontier' themes of dangerous threats and hopeful opportunities continue to be balanced against each other. The famously unlimited commitment to liberty's survival and success was an important Cold War moment and owed much to the need that Kennedy felt to assert himself as a serious and knowledgeable statesman. At 43 he was the youngest president ever elected, and the international stage at that time was still dominated by the older generation of Nikita Khrushchev, Harold Macmillan, Charles de Gaulle and Konrad Adenauer. The inaugural address therefore turns youth and energy into qualifications for high office, and the idea of a briskly scene-setting first '100 days' in power captivated political practitioners and commentators alike. Kennedy's spare literary style was the perfect medium to express this business-like commitment to the job in hand. He belonged to a period when politicians were not expected to express their inner emotions or to empathize with the electorate by offering suitably edited highlights from their personal experiences. This is a strikingly dispassionate speech. But by avoiding the ponderous Kennedy achieved a sparse lyricism, and the constitutional truths of the late 18th century are re-expressed with a contemporary freshness and relevance.

The remarks addressed to 'our sister republics south of our border' had a special relevance for Cuba, then two years into its government by Fidel Castro's regime, as well as for the USSR, whose close Cuban involvement was now well documented. But Kennedy also outlined his government's commitment to the principle of negotiation and cooperation in order to reduce international tensions with the Soviets and their allies. There is a clear recognition of the link between political stability and economic progress, and an eloquent understanding of the dangers posed by the persistence of Third World poverty. The enterprise to which the new president had summoned his fellow citizens was undeniably grand – as well as one couched in terms of a traditional American trust in the individualizing virtues of self-reliance. But this was also a truly international moment, an assertion of America's leadership in both ethical and political terms, and a rejection of the idea that the US could be either isolationist or unilateralist when responding to the urgency of the present.

'

We observe today not a victory of party, but a celebration of freedom – symbolizing an end as well as a beginning, signifying renewal as well as change. For I have sworn before you and almighty God the same solemn oath our forebears prescribed nearly a century and three-quarters ago.

The world is very different now. For man holds in his mortal hands the power to abolish all forms of human poverty and all forms of human life. And yet the same revolutionary beliefs for which our forebears fought are still at issue around the globe – the belief that the rights of man come not from the generosity of the state but from the hand of God.

'Man holds in his mortal hands the power to abolish all forms of human poverty and all forms of human life'

We dare not forget today that we are the heirs of that first revolution. Let the word go forth from this time and place, to friend and foe alike, that the torch has been passed to a new generation of Americans – born in this century, tempered by war, disciplined by a hard and bitter peace, proud of our ancient heritage, and unwilling to witness or permit the slow undoing of those human rights to which this nation has always been committed, and to which we are committed today at home and around the world. Let every nation know, whether it wishes us well or ill, that we shall pay any price, bear any burden, meet any hardship, support any friend, oppose any foe, to assure the survival and the success of liberty . . .

To those old allies whose cultural and spiritual origins we share, we pledge the loyalty of faithful friends . . .

To those new states whom we welcome to the ranks of the free, we pledge our word that one form of colonial control shall not have passed away merely to be replaced by a far more iron tyranny . . .

'Let the word go forth from this time and place, to friend and foe alike, that the torch has been passed to a new generation of Americans'

To those people in the huts and villages of half the globe struggling to break the bonds of mass misery, we pledge our best efforts to help them help themselves, for whatever period is required – not because the communists may be doing it, not because we seek their votes, but because it is right . . .

Ask not what your country can do for you;
ask what you can do for your country'

To our sister republics south of our border, we offer a special pledge: to convert our good words into good deeds in a new alliance for progress, to assist free men and free governments in casting off the chains of poverty. But this peaceful revolution of hope cannot become the prey of hostile powers. Let all our neighbours know that we shall join with them to oppose aggression or subversion anywhere in the Americas. And let every other power know that this hemisphere intends to remain the master of its own house.

To that world assembly of sovereign states, the United Nations . . . we renew our pledge of support – to prevent it from becoming merely a forum for invective, to strengthen its shield of the new and the weak, and to enlarge the area in which its writ may run.

Finally, to those nations who would make themselves our adversary, we offer not a pledge but a request: that both sides begin anew the quest for peace . . . Only when our arms are sufficient beyond doubt can we be certain beyond doubt that they will never be employed.

But neither can two great and powerful groups of nations take comfort from our present course – both sides overburdened by the cost of modern weapons, both rightly alarmed by the steady spread of the deadly atom . . .

'Together let us explore the stars, conquer the deserts, eradicate disease, tap the ocean depths, and encourage the arts and commerce'

So let us begin anew – remembering on both sides that civility is not a sign of weakness, and sincerity is always subject to proof. Let us never negotiate out of fear, but let us never fear to negotiate . . .

Let both sides, for the first time, formulate serious and precise proposals for the inspection and control of arms, and bring the absolute power to destroy other nations under the absolute control of all nations . . .

Together let us explore the stars, conquer the deserts, eradicate disease, tap the ocean depths, and encourage the arts and commerce. Let both sides unite to heed, in all corners of the earth, the command of Isaiah – to 'undo the heavy burdens, and let the oppressed go free'. And if a beachhead of cooperation may push back the jungle of suspicion, let both sides join in creating . . . a new world of law, where the strong are just and the weak secure and the peace preserved.

All this will not be finished in the first 100 days. Nor will it be finished in the first 1000 days, nor in the life of this administration, nor even perhaps in our lifetime on this planet. But let us begin.

In your hands, my fellow citizens, more than mine, will rest the final success or failure of our course. Since this country was founded, each generation of Americans has been summoned to give testimony to its national loyalty . . . Now the trumpet summons us again – not as a call to arms, though arms we need; not as a call to battle, though embattled we are; but a call to bear the burden of a long twilight struggle, year in and year out . . . a struggle against the common enemies of man: tyranny, poverty, disease and war itself . . .

> *'Ask not . . . what America will do for you,*
> *but what, together, we can do for*
> *the freedom of man'*

In the long history of the world, only a few generations have been granted the role of defending freedom in its hour of maximum danger. I do not shrink from this responsibility – I welcome it. I do not believe that any of us would exchange places with any other people or any other generation . . . And so, my fellow Americans, ask not what your country can do for you; ask what you can do for your country. My fellow citizens of the world, ask not what America will do for you, but what, together, we can do for the freedom of man . . .

With a good conscience our only sure reward, with history the final judge of our deeds, let us go forth to lead the land we love, asking His blessing and His help, but knowing that here on earth God's work must truly be our own.

'Mankind must put an end to war – or war will put an end to mankind'

John F. Kennedy

(1917–63)

**THE US PRESIDENT STRESSES THE URGENCY OF LIMITING NUCLEAR TESTING;
UN GENERAL ASSEMBLY, NEW YORK CITY, 25 SEPTEMBER 1961**

Kennedy was addressing an institution in crisis, a week after the death of Dag Hammarskjöld, a figure of unique authority in UN history. The general secretary had been killed in a plane crash while attempting mediation in the Congolese civil war, and in the ensuing vacuum doubts were raised about the UN's rationale. Kennedy's speech boosted its self-confidence and recalled the UN to urgent work on the control of nuclear testing as part of the more general goal of slowing down the arms race.

The US's successful test on 1 November 1952 of a hydrogen bomb – one based on the principle of staged radiation implosion – led to widespread fears about the effect of nuclear fallout on the planet's atmosphere. Western nuclear powers and the USSR therefore started to negotiate a test ban, but by 1961 these talks, presided over by the UN Disarmament Commission, had stalled. Kennedy's speech highlighted the issue's importance, and subsequent progress involved separating the question of nuclear disarmament from that of nuclear testing.

US, UK and Soviet government representatives signed the Partial Test Ban Treaty in Moscow on 5 August 1963, after which other countries could decide whether to follow suit. Most did so, though France and China were important exceptions. The treaty prohibits its signatories from conducting nuclear testing on the ground, in the atmosphere and underwater. Britain and the US maintained, however, that underground testing, to be effective, needed a neutral system of inspection based within the country concerned. The USSR disagreed, but in July 1963 President Khrushchev accepted that the treaty would have to exclude a ban on underground testing.

Kennedy remained the Cold War politician who in his inaugural address in January 1961 committed the US to 'pay any price . . . to assure the survival and the success of liberty'. In this speech he still thought his country should send arms and 'join free men in standing up to their responsibilities'. But his words here are tempered by experience of office and by a novel fear of the abyss, with the Bay of Pigs expedition (April 1961) providing a recent revelation of defects in US intelligence and military planning. A force of Cuban exiles, armed by the US, had hoped to oust Castro but were mown down when they landed in the bay. Ahead lay the Cuban Missile Crisis and its demonstration of how irrationality, fear and ignorance might upset the nuclear balancing act.

The speech expresses a major theme of the presidency: peace was 'primarily a problem of politics and people', and it therefore involved the human skills of negotiation. A federally funded Peace Corps composed of US civilian volunteers had been established just days before Kennedy spoke, and its provision of trained manpower working on Third World development projects formed an important part of his global vision. Kennedy's precisely formulated goals in this speech helped set the agenda for disarmament talks in the next quarter of a century, a time of intermittent hope that the great powers might be able to negotiate themselves out of a world crisis.

'Mankind must put an end to war – or war will put an end to mankind'

'

Unconditional war can no longer lead to unconditional victory. It can no longer serve to settle disputes . . . Mankind must put an end to war – or war will put an end to mankind . . .

Today, every inhabitant of the planet must contemplate the day when this planet may no longer be habitable . . . Men may no longer pretend that the quest for disarmament is a sign of weakness – for in a spiralling arms race, a nation's security may well be shrinking even as its arms increase . . .

'In a spiralling arms race, a nation's security may well be shrinking even as its arms increase'

It is therefore our intention to challenge the Soviet Union, not to an arms race, but to a peace race – to advance together step by step, stage by stage, until general and complete disarmament has been achieved.

The programme . . . would place the final responsibility for verification and control . . . in an international organization within the framework of the United Nations. It would assure . . . true inspection and apply it in stages proportionate to the stage of disarmament. It would cover delivery systems as well as weapons. It would ultimately halt their production as well as their testing, their transfer as well as their possession . . .

Such a plan would not bring a world free from conflict and greed, but it would bring a world free from the terrors of mass destruction. It would not usher in the era of the super state, but it would usher in an era in which no state could annihilate or be annihilated by another . . .

To halt the spread of these terrible weapons, to halt the contamination of the air, to halt the spiralling nuclear arms race, our new Disarmament Programme thus includes the following proposals:

– First, signing the test-ban treaty by all nations.

– Second, stopping the production of fissionable materials for use in weapons, and preventing their transfer to any nation now lacking in nuclear weapons.

– Third, prohibiting the transfer of control over nuclear weapons to states that do not own them.

– Fourth, keeping nuclear weapons from seeding new battlegrounds in outer space.

– Fifth, gradually destroying existing nuclear weapons and converting their materials to peaceful uses; and

– Finally, halting the unlimited testing and production of strategic nuclear delivery vehicles, and gradually destroying them as well.

To destroy arms, however, is not enough. We must create even as we destroy – creating worldwide law and law enforcement as we outlaw worldwide war and weapons . . .

Therefore, the United States recommends that all member nations earmark special peace-keeping units in their armed forces – to be on call of the United Nations . . . and with advanced provision for financial and logistic support . . .

For peace is not solely a matter of military or technical problems – it is primarily a problem of politics and people. And unless man can match his strides in weaponry and technology with equal strides in social and political development, our great strength, like that of the dinosaur, will become incapable of proper control – and like the dinosaur vanish from the earth.

As we extend the rule of law on earth, so must we also extend it to man's new domain – outer space . . . The cold reaches of the universe must not become the new arena of an even colder war.

To this end, we shall urge proposals . . . reserving outer space for peaceful use, prohibiting weapons of mass destruction in space or on celestial bodies, and opening the mysteries and benefits of space to every nation. We shall propose . . . a global system of communication satellites linking the whole world in telegraph and telephone and radio and television . . .

'My nation was once a colony, and we know what colonialism means'

Political sovereignty is but a mockery without the means of meeting poverty and illiteracy and disease. Self-determination is but a slogan if the future holds no hope . . . New research, technical assistance and pilot projects can unlock the wealth of less developed lands and untapped waters. And development can become a cooperative and not a competitive enterprise – to enable all nations . . . to become in fact as well as in law free and equal . . .

I do not ignore the remaining problems of traditional colonialism which still confront this body. But colonialism in its harshest forms is not only the exploitation of new nations by old, of dark skins by light, or the subjugation of the poor by the rich. My nation was once a colony, and we know what colonialism means; the exploitation and subjugation of the weak by the powerful, of the many by the few, of the governed who have given no consent to be governed . . .

And that is why there is no ignoring the fact that the tide of self-determination has not reached the communist empire where a population lives under governments installed by foreign troops . . . under a system which knows only one party . . . and which builds a wall to keep truth a stranger and its own citizens prisoners . . .

'The United States has both the will and the weapons to join free men in standing up to their responsibilities.'

Terror is not a new weapon. Throughout history it has been used by those who could not prevail, either by persuasion or example. But inevitably they fail, either because men are not afraid to die for a life worth living, or because the terrorists themselves came to realize that free men cannot be frightened by threats and that aggression would meet its own response. And it is in the light of that history that every nation today should know, be he friend or foe, that the United States has both the will and the weapons to join free men in standing up to their responsibilities . . .

We in this hall shall be remembered either as part of the generation that turned this planet into a flaming pyre or the generation that met its vow 'to save succeeding generations from the scourge of war'. In the endeavour to meet that vow, I pledge you . . . that we shall never negotiate out of fear, we shall never fear to negotiate . . .

'Together we shall save our planet, or together we shall perish in its flames'

Never have the nations of the world had so much to lose, or so much to gain. Together we shall save our planet, or together we shall perish in its flames. Save it we can – and save it we must – and then we shall earn the eternal thanks of mankind and, as peacemakers, the eternal blessing of God.

'*There is no independence imaginable for a country that does not have its own nuclear weapon*'

Charles de Gaulle

(1890–1970)

THE FRENCH PRESIDENT INSISTS ON FRANCE'S NEED FOR ITS OWN
NUCLEAR WEAPONS; ÉCOLE MILITAIRE,
PARIS, 15 FEBRUARY 1963

'There is no independence imaginable for a country that does not have its own nuclear weapon'

In 1963 the wounds inflicted on France's authority and reputation during the Algerian War of Independence remained raw. The French colony witnessed atrocities committed on both sides following the rebellion's outbreak in 1954, and four years later French officers based in Algiers led a military insurrection. Condemning their government for irresolute handling of the war, the dissidents called for de Gaulle's return to power. France's Fourth Republic was dissolved and the new constitution strengthened the authority of the presidency – the office to which de Gaulle was elected in November 1958 after exercising emergency powers as premier in the preceding six months. Having decided that suppression of Algerian nationalism was not feasible politically, de Gaulle changed tack and the national referendum of French voters held in January 1961 approved his plan for an independent Algeria. Right-wing elements within France and Algerian colonists were equally outraged. In an effort to reverse the policy, four retired generals organized a putsch which attempted the seizure of Paris and of Algeria's major cities in April 1961. Although it failed and Algeria became independent in 1962, the conspiracy showed a depth of feeling against de Gaulle within the army, and his critics associated the general's volte-face with a subversion of French national honour.

De Gaulle was speaking at France's elite military academy, and it was important that he should both inspire a demoralized army and move the national agenda on. The emphases are typically Gaullist: the invocation of France's destiny, nationality and independence, and the assertion of a personal link between the general and his country's fortunes. His instinct for the big historical picture – with France firmly in the foreground – is evident in his remarks on the evolution of weaponry and its relationship to differing forms of state power.

CHARLES DE GAULLE (1890–1970)

1912 Graduates from St-Cyr Military Academy; commissioned as an officer in the 33rd Infantry Regiment of the French army.

March 1916 Wounded at Battle of Verdun and taken prisoner.

1934 Publishes *The Army of the Future*, urging mechanization of the army and more mobile strategies in warfare.

18 June 1940 Broadcasts from London his 'Appeal' urging the French people to resist the German army's occupation.

1940–4 Leader of the Free French.

1944–6 Prime minister, French provisional government.

June 1958 Returns as premier, exercising emergency powers.

Jan 1959 Takes office as elected president of France.

May 1968 Student demonstrators disrupt central Paris.

April 1969 Resigns the presidency.

France became the world's fourth nuclear power in 1960 after detonating an atomic bomb in the Algerian desert, and de Gaulle's pursuit of an independent defence policy was designed to bolster French prestige and self-belief. This strenuous programme also had the political advantage of keeping the French military so busy that it had little time to dwell on Algeria and nurse grudges. Suspicion of the close links between the US and the UK determined de Gaulle's scepticism about NATO – an organization he considered subservient to the two allies' interests – and in 1966 France's armed forces were withdrawn from NATO's integrated command structure, though the country retained its membership of the military alliance. West Germany's membership of NATO was a further problem, in his view, since it made the country especially vulnerable to invasion from the communist powers to its east. This was the possible 'battle of Germany' here referred to and de Gaulle feared that France would then be drawn into a global war between NATO and Warsaw Pact forces. In that eventuality, he wished to maintain the option of concluding a separate peace between France and the Eastern bloc, a possibility strengthened by advertising his disagreement with NATO. French independence was basic to his vision of a 'free Europe', a third power bloc acting as a counterweight to the US and the USSR.

There is no point concealing from you the emotion I feel at finding myself, once more in my life, here where in the past I have had so many occasions to encounter ideas, participate in work, engage in reflections which have undoubtedly contributed in great measure to the tasks I have subsequently been called upon to perform in the service of France . . .

Nor do I wish to conceal from you the satisfaction I have felt in meeting you all, that is to say all the various branches of staff college training and the National Defence Institute . . .

Wherever I have passed among you, I have encountered in your work and in your concerns the overwhelming issue of the day, by which I mean nuclear weapons . . . It is only natural that I should explain to you . . . the underlying conceptions guiding the head of state and the government in the matter of defence as they see it, and as they are responsible for organizing and, potentially, directing it.Long ago, the emergence of metal weapons gave birth to the great hegemonies of antiquity. After them came the barbarian invasions and the feudal system that followed. Then the advent of fire-arms made possible the rebirth of centralized states. This resulted in the great wars, the wars of Europe, where each of the great powers of the period sought to dominate in turn: Spain, England, France, Turkey, Germany, Russia. The emergence of fire-arms also sparked off and made possible colonization, in other words the conquest of vast regions: America, India, the East, Africa.

Finally, the power of the motor emerged as a factor in combat, by sea, air and land. It was this that made it possible to bring the First World War to an end. It was this that furnished the conquering ambition of Nazi Germany with an instrument. It was this that also gave the free world what was required to crush that ambition.

'There is no independence imaginable for a country that does not have its own nuclear weapon'

Today, the development of nuclear weapons has in its turn brought about a complete upheaval in terms of security, and hence the policies, of states, even in times of peace. The upheaval would be all the greater in time of war. Imagination itself cannot encompass what might be the consequences of the use of nuclear weapons, except to realize that, in any event, such a use would lead to a total subversion in human society . . .

> *'Imagination itself cannot encompass what might be the consequences of the use of nuclear weapons'*

Under such circumstances it is clear that there is no independence imaginable for a country that does not have its own nuclear weapon, because if it does not have such a weapon it will be forced to rely for its security, and consequently for its policy, on another country which does. It is true that certain countries of the world imagine that they can wrap themselves in neutrality . . . believing that in this way they will be overlooked by destiny. In reality, however, they will only be able to await their fate without being in any way able to alter it.

For France, whose geographical situation, whose historical raison d'être and political nature all rule out neutrality, for France which has no intention of handing over responsibility for her own fate to a foreign nation, no matter how friendly, it is absolutely necessary that she should have the wherewithal to act in any war, in other words that she should have nuclear arms.

The question of whether the total power of those arms will be equal to the total power of the arms of any adversary, and the question of whether our country could prosecute a global conflict without alliances – and, clearly, the answer to both those questions must be negative – in no way alters the elementary need for us to have our own nuclear weapons, to employ them, if necessary, as we see fit and, equally naturally, to combine the use of such weapons with the analogous weapons of our allies as part of a common effort.

These are the principles. How might they be applied?

The existence of nuclear weapons . . . causes an immense uncertainty to hover over all battles, over their nature, their rhythm, their development. If an exchange of strategic nuclear weapons between two camps . . . is capable of causing the destruction of those two states, it follows that . . . there is absolutely no way to predict if, why, where, when, how or to what extent the two nations, assured of mutual destruction, might wish to trigger such an exchange . . .

'We are resolved . . . not to be annihilated as a state and as a nation without having defended our homeland'

If the battle of Germany, the first battle in the war, went badly, whether it were to any degree a nuclear battle or not at all, the immediate consequence would be the destruction or the invasion of France and, at the same time, the loss of any bridgehead for the free world in Europe. We, however, are resolved, whatever may happen, not to be annihilated as a state and as a nation without having defended our homeland, body and soul, on the ground, and we are further convinced that in so doing we would create a chance of final victory.

All of these considerations therefore prompt us to possess our own nuclear arms at our own disposal for any nuclear strike. They prompt us also to possess the means of intervening, on land, sea and in the air, wherever circumstances would appear to us to dictate, and to possess the means of offering national resistance to the invader on our own territory . . .

'All of these considerations therefore prompt us to possess our own nuclear arms'

Such are the conceptions which have led the head of state and the government to draw up the defence plan, the organization plan and the arms plan currently in force or in preparation . . . These necessities are imposing on the French command structure a new era of initiative, authority and responsibility. For those who would have the honour of commanding in the midst of cataclysm . . . the role and duty of staff college training are essential . . . in holding themselves ready intellectually, morally and technically.

I have confidence in you, gentlemen, and in the commanders responsible for leading you, to fulfil this role and accomplish this duty.

Gentlemen, I have the honour to salute you.

'I have a dream'
Martin Luther King, Jr
(1929–68)

THE GREAT CIVIL RIGHTS CHAMPION SPEAKS AT THE MARCH ON WASHINGTON
FOR JOBS AND FREEDOM; LINCOLN MEMORIAL,
WASHINGTON, 28 AUGUST 1963

Over 200,000 people had gathered in the damp savannah heat of a Washington summer's day to hear Dr Martin Luther King, Jr speak of the conquest of prejudice and the fulfilment of prophecy. The year 1963 was the centenary of the Emancipation Declaration, the edict which had been signed by Abraham Lincoln and whose provisions had freed the slaves of the Confederate states during their rebellion against the Union. The civil rights movement against racial prejudice had now broadened into a campaign against black poverty and unemployment, which is why the crowds addressed by King in the capital were part of a 'March on Washington for Jobs and Freedom'.

Assembled before the memorial to Lincoln, the marchers stood in his 'symbolic shadow' since black Americans, though emancipated in law, were still subjected to 'the chains of discrimination' in areas such as education, housing and employment. King's analogy with a bounced cheque was typically deft. The founding fathers of the US had signed the equivalent of a 'promissory note' when approving the text of the original Constitution and Declaration of Independence. But America had defaulted on this note 'in so far as her citizens of colour are concerned'. King suggests that the country's wealth is spiritual and intellectual as well as material, and that the bankruptcy of her 'bank of justice' is therefore a notion defying credibility. America was being reminded of her own best self and of the need to live up to her proclaimed goals of freedom and opportunity. King spoke therefore as an American whose own personal dream for his family and people was grounded in the reality of the 'American dream' as a whole. Much of the speech's impact was due to its emphasis on this collective experience of the nation and the shared destiny of its people.

King also spoke here as a Baptist minister intellectually grounded in biblical theology, in the protests of Old Testament prophets against unjust rulers and in the New Testament account of redemption through forgiveness. And the cadences of his delivery owed everything to his training in the technique of the Protestant sermon, with its emphasis on argument and its use of the illustrative example drawn from personal

MARTIN LUTHER KING (1929–68)

1955 Receives PhD in theology from Boston University.

1955–6 Leads Montgomery bus boycott in protest against racial segregation.

Aug 1963 Co-leader of March on Washington for Jobs and Freedom.

1964 Wins Nobel Peace Prize.

April 1967 Delivers 'Beyond Vietnam' speech in protest against US involvement in Vietnam.

April 1968 Assassinated in Memphis, Tennessee.

experience. Although approaching sublimity in content and delivery, King's oratory was never remote from his audience or congregation. In this speech he describes the journey which will take black Americans out of the ghetto and at the end of which 'justice rolls down like waters and righteousness like a mighty stream'. The imagery is biblical and exalted but the passage is introduced by a fact of daily life: the colour bar which frustrated the travels of black Americans by excluding them from certain motels and hotels. The urgency of the present crisis is captured by King's typical emphasis on heightened contrasts. Segregation's darkness in states such as Alabama and Mississippi, Georgia and Tennessee is defined by its remoteness from 'the sunlit path of racial justice'. But the concluding peroration offers an inclusive message, one which transcends the old and rings in the new.

Five score years ago, a great American, in whose symbolic shadow we stand, signed the Emancipation Proclamation. This momentous decree came as a great beacon light of hope to millions of Negro slaves who had been seared in the flames of withering injustice . . .

But one hundred years later, we must face the tragic fact that the Negro is still not free. One hundred years later, the life of the Negro is still sadly crippled by the manacles of segregation and the chains of discrimination. One hundred years later, the Negro lives on a lonely island of poverty in the midst of a vast ocean of material prosperity. One hundred years later, the Negro . . . finds himself an exile in his own land . . .

'The life of the Negro is still sadly crippled by the manacles of segregation and the chains of discrimination'

When the architects of our republic wrote the magnificent words of the Constitution and the Declaration of Independence, they were signing a promissory note to which every American was to fall heir. This note was a promise that all men would be guaranteed the inalienable rights of life, liberty and the pursuit of happiness.

It is obvious today that America has defaulted on this promissory note in so far as her citizens of colour are concerned. But we refuse to believe that the bank of justice is bankrupt. We refuse to believe that there are insufficient funds in the great vaults of opportunity of this nation . . .

Now is the time to rise from the dark and desolate valley of segregation to the sunlit path of racial justice. Now is the time to lift our nation from the quicksands of racial injustice to the solid rock of brotherhood . . .

The formation of Umkhonto we Sizwe (Spear of the Nation), the armed wing of the previously non-violent African National Congress (ANC), marked a new and decisive stage in the history of South Africa's anti-apartheid movement. On 21 March 1960, 20,000 blacks had gathered outside the police station in the Johannesburg suburb of Sharpeville to protest against the pass laws which restricted their rights of movement within the country's overwhelmingly white urban areas. Police fired at the crowd, killing some 70 protesters and wounding many more, and the ensuing crisis created an acute problem of leadership for the ANC.

A new generation of black activists had emerged in the townships, those areas on the urban peripheries reserved for non-whites, and from the 1950s onwards they were urging a more vigorous assault on white supremacy. The ANC establishment, feeling threatened, had built alliances with other dissident groups, including communists, among South Africa's white, 'coloured' (racially mixed) and Indian communities. Having been banned after Sharpeville, the ANC then sought to reassert its authority in the eyes of black South Africans and to demonstrate its continued command of the strategic impetus. The establishment of an armed organization was part of this plan and the initial bombing campaign sought to sabotage South Africa's infrastructure and its military and industrial installations, rather than to take human life. Umkhonto would, however, adopt urban guerrilla warfare to bloody effect during the years of Nelson Mandela's imprisonment. In his earlier years Mandela had advocated Gandhi's methods of pacific protest, but as a co-founder and leader of Umkhonto he coordinated the sabotage programme and raised foreign funds for the campaign. He also organized paramilitary training in anticipation of the need for

NELSON ROLIHLAHLA MANDELA (b. 1918)

1912 South African Native National Congress established (subsequently African National Congress, or ANC).

1937 Enrolls at Healdtown, a Wesleyan Methodist school in Eastern Cape province; subsequently follows the University of South Africa's correspondence courses and studies law at the University of Witwatersrand.

1943 Joins ANC.

1948 Afrikaaner-dominated National Party wins general election on a manifesto pledged to systematic apartheid.

1955 Congress of the People: a summit at which the ANC adopts chief elements of its anti-apartheid programme.

5 Dec 1956 Arrested with 150 others on a charge of treason; all are acquitted after a five-year trial.

1961 Co-founds Umkhonto.

25 Oct 1962 Sentenced to five years' imprisonment.

Dec 1963–June 1964 The Rivonia trial.

Timeline continues on page 171

'An ideal for which I am prepared to die'

outright warfare, should the sabotage offensive fail to convert an intransigent government.

At the time of his trial Mandela was already serving a five-year prison sentence imposed in 1962 on charges of leading a strike and leaving the country without permission. While he was imprisoned, other ANC leaders were arrested at a farmhouse in Rivonia, a Johannesburg suburb. At the 'Rivonia trial' charges of committing sabotage and planning acts of treason were brought against 11 of these activists. Mandela was indicted on the same counts and joined these defendants in the dock. Two of the accused managed to escape from prison while on remand. Mandela was among the eight sentenced to life imprisonment in 1964, and he was sent to Robben Island prison.

In presenting the case for his defence Mandela had the advantage of a legal mind trained in the presentation and assessment of evidence. Although facing a possible death sentence – which had been demanded by the prosecution – he presents a reasoned and dispassionate account of his motives and actions. Even when describing the oppression and poverty of South Africa's non-whites, it is the facts that matter to Mandela, and they were eloquent enough in themselves. That same quality of dispassion would enable him to rise above his immediate circumstances in the long years of captivity that lay ahead.

I admit immediately that I was one of the persons who helped to form Umkhonto we Sizwe . . . All lawful modes of expressing opposition had been closed by legislation, and we were placed in a position in which we had either to accept a permanent state of inferiority, or to defy the government . . .

In 1960 there was the shooting at Sharpeville, which resulted in the proclamation of a state of emergency and the declaration of the ANC as an unlawful organization. My colleagues and I, after careful consideration, decided that we would not obey this decree. The African people were not part of the government and did not make the laws by which they were governed. The ANC refused to dissolve, but instead went underground . . .

'The country was drifting towards a civil war in which blacks and whites would fight each other'

It could not be denied that our policy to achieve a non-racial state by non-violence had achieved nothing, and that our followers were losing confidence in this policy and were developing disturbing ideas of terrorism . . . Already small groups had arisen in the urban areas and were spontaneously making plans for violent forms of political struggle. There now arose a danger that these groups would adopt terrorism against Africans, as well as whites, if not properly directed . . .

We felt that the country was drifting towards a civil war in which blacks and whites would fight each other . . . We did not want to be committed to civil war, but we wanted to be ready if it became inevitable . . . Sabotage did not involve loss of life, and it offered the best hope for future race relations . . . We believed that South Africa depended to a large extent on foreign capital and foreign trade. We felt that planned destruction of power plants, and interference with rail and telephone communications, would tend to scare away capital from the country . . . thus compelling the voters of the country to reconsider their position. Attacks on the economic life lines of the country were to be linked with sabotage on government buildings and other symbols of apartheid. These attacks would serve as a source of inspiration to our people . . .

The manifesto of Umkhonto was issued on the day that operations commenced . . . The whites failed to respond by suggesting change . . . In contrast, the response of the Africans was one of encouragement. Suddenly there was hope again . . . But we in Umkhonto weighed up the white response with anxiety. The lines were being drawn . . . We decided, therefore, in our preparations for the future, to make provision for the possibility of guerrilla warfare . . . I started to make a study of the art of war and revolution and, whilst abroad, underwent a course in military training . . .

Another of the allegations made by the state is that the aims and objects of the ANC and the Communist Party are the same . . . The ANC has never at any period of its history advocated a revolutionary change in the economic structure of the country, nor has it ever condemned capitalist society . . . It is true that there has often been close cooperation between the ANC and the Communist Party. But cooperation is merely proof of a common goal – in this case the removal of white supremacy – and is not proof of a complete community of interests . . . Theoretical differences amongst those fighting against oppression is a luxury we cannot afford at this stage . . .

'We fight against two features which are the hallmark of African life in South Africa'

From my reading of Marxist literature, I have gained the impression that communists regard the parliamentary system of the West as undemocratic and reactionary. But . . . I have great respect for British political institutions and for the country's system of justice. I regard the British parliament as the most democratic institution in the world, and the independence and impartiality of its judiciary never fails to arouse my admiration. The American Congress, that country's doctrine of separation of powers, as well as the independence of its judiciary, arouses in me similar sentiments . . .

Basically we fight against two features which are the hallmark of African life in South

Africa and which are entrenched by legislation. These features are poverty and lack of human dignity, and we do not need 'communists' or so-called 'agitators' to teach us about these things.

'White supremacy implies black inferiority'

South Africa is the richest country in Africa . . . but it is a land of extremes and remarkable contrasts. The whites enjoy what may well be the highest standard of living in the world, whilst Africans live in poverty and misery . . . The complaint of Africans, however, is not only that they are poor and the whites rich, but that the laws which are made by the whites are designed to preserve this situation . . .

White supremacy implies black inferiority . . . whites tend to regard Africans as a separate breed. They do not look upon them as people with families of their own; they do not realize that they have emotions – that they fall in love like white people do . . . that they want to earn enough money to support their families properly . . .

Hundreds and thousands of Africans are thrown into jail each year under pass laws. Even worse than this is the fact that pass laws keep husband and wife apart and lead to the breakdown of family life . . . Children wander about the streets of the townships because they have no school to go to . . . or no parents at home to see that they go to school, because both parents (if there be two) have to work to keep the family alive. This leads to a breakdown in moral standards, to an alarming rise in illegitimacy, and to growing violence . . .

'I have fought against white domination, and I have fought against black domination'

Africans . . . want equal political rights, because without them our disabilities will be permanent . . . It is not true that the enfranchisement of all will result in racial domination . . . The ANC has spent half a century fighting against racialism. When it triumphs, it will not change that policy . . .

I have fought against white domination, and I have fought against black domination. I have cherished the ideal of a democratic and free society in which all persons live together in harmony and with equal opportunities. It is an ideal which I hope to live for and to achieve. But if needs be, it is an ideal for which I am prepared to die.

'Extremism in the defence of liberty is no vice . . . moderation in the pursuit of justice is no virtue'

Barry Goldwater

(1909–98)

SPEECH ACCEPTING THE REPUBLICAN PARTY'S PRESIDENTIAL NOMINATION,
DELIVERED AT THE REPUBLICAN NATIONAL CONVENTION,
SAN FRANCISCO, 16 JULY 1964

*'Extremism in the defence of liberty is no vice . . . moderation
in the pursuit of justice is no virtue'*

He rejoiced in the title of 'Mr Conservative' but this speech ended Barry Goldwater's hopes of being called 'Mr President'. This ringing flow of words is unique in America's political history, and the crisp delivery of its unambiguous message marked Goldwater out as a true original who rose above the platitudes of consensus politics. The object of his ire was twofold: the communist threat to both the US and democratic values worldwide; and the expansion of federal activity which, ever since F.D. Roosevelt's introduction of assorted 'New Deal' programmes, had transformed American lives and opinions. An inadequate response to the former, a supine acceptance of the latter: these had, in Goldwater's view, sapped the nation's moral fibre. This was not so much a politician as a prophet who, it seemed, had emerged out of Arizona's desert intent on rebuking an America which had fallen from its erstwhile state of grace. Goldwater's austerely bespectacled expression appeared to provide confirmation of a trigger-happy zealotry.

Prolonged acclamation followed the observation – lifted from Cicero and loosely rendered – to the effect that 'extremism in the defence of liberty is no vice'. But a politician's words to his disciples can turn into his opponents' useful weapons, and from now on Goldwater could be labelled a dangerous extremist who might start a nuclear war. 'In your heart you know he's right' ran the Republican campaign slogan – with the Democrats scripting the riposte: 'In your guts you know he's nuts.' His speech made Goldwater appear anarchic rather than just conservative, and Karl Heiss, the anti-state activist who scripted most of it, would later be charged with tax resistance by the Internal Revenue Service.

In that November's election Goldwater got only 38 per cent of the popular vote and carried, apart from Arizona, just five states. But Alabama, Georgia, Louisiana, Mississippi and South Carolina had all been Democrat previously, and his campaign marked the beginning of a profound political and ideological shift. The American South, previously

BARRY GOLDWATER (1909–98)

1930 Takes over running of family business, a department store in Phoenix, Arizona.

1942–5 Serves in US Air Force, attaining rank of major general.

1952 Wins US Senate seat for Arizona; re-elected in 1958.

1964 Becomes the Republican presidential candidate; loses November presidential election to Democratic incumbent Lyndon B. Johnson.

1968 Re-elected senator for Arizona, and again in 1974 and 1980.

Jan 1987 Retires from the US Senate, having served as chair of the Senate Intelligence and Armed Service Committee in his final term.

dominated by Democrats, would become the electoral base of a Republican Party enthused by many of Goldwater's stances. Republicans who adhered to the political centre, such as New York's governor Nelson Rockefeller, were sidelined and the party's representation in the northeast of the country withered away. In 1964 Republicans remained divided rather than converted en masse – hence Goldwater's reference to their discord – and Rockefeller came close to gaining the nomination. But the future belonged to Goldwater's heirs, and the presidencies of Ronald Reagan, George Bush and George W. Bush are inconceivable without his prior work as one of 'freedom's missionaries'.

He remained, though, intellectually independent, rather than a slave to party orthodoxy, and a libertarian defence of the individual conscience lent a grandly rugged unity to his career. Goldwater's radicalism flared up again late in life when he criticized the ban on gays serving in the military and voted in the Senate to uphold legalized abortion. Evangelical right-wing Christians were by then a forceful element within the electoral coalition which had swept his party to power, but the intolerance of those he labelled 'a bunch of kooks' appalled his nonconforming soul.

The Good Lord raised this mighty Republic to be a home for the brave and to flourish as the land of the free – not to stagnate in the swampland of collectivism, not to cringe before the bully of communism . . .

Our people have followed false prophets. We must, and we shall, return to proven ways – not because they are old, but because they are true. We must, and we shall, set the tide running again in the cause of freedom. And this party . . . has but a single resolve, and that is freedom – freedom made orderly for this nation by our constitutional government; freedom under a government limited by laws of nature and of nature's God; freedom – balanced so that liberty lacking order will not become the slavery of the prison cell; balanced so that liberty lacking order will not become the licence of the mob and of the jungle . . .

'Absolute power does corrupt, and those who seek it must be suspect and must be opposed'

We can be freedom's missionaries in a doubting world. But first we must renew freedom's mission in our own hearts . . .

We have lost the brisk pace of diversity and the genius of individual creativity. We are plodding at a pace set by centralized planning, red tape, rules without responsibility and regimentation without recourse . . .

Those who seek to live your lives for you, to take your liberties in return for relieving

'Extremism in the defence of liberty is no vice . . . moderation
in the pursuit of justice is no virtue'

you of yours, those who elevate the state and downgrade the citizen must see ultimately a world in which earthly power can be substituted for divine will, and this nation was founded upon the rejection of that notion and upon the acceptance of God as the author of freedom.

Those who seek absolute power, even though they seek it to do what they regard as good, are simply demanding the right to enforce their own version of heaven on earth. And . . . they are the very ones who always create the most hellish tyrannies. Absolute power does corrupt, and those who seek it must be suspect and must be opposed. Their mistaken course stems from false notions of equality. Equality, rightly understood, . . . leads to liberty and to the emancipation of creative differences. Wrongly understood . . . it leads first to conformity and then to despotism . . .

It is the cause of Republicanism to resist concentrations of power, private or public, which enforce such conformity and inflict such despotism . . . It is our cause to dispel the foggy thinking which avoids hard decisions in the illusion that a world of conflict will somehow mysteriously resolve itself into a world of harmony . . .

'Only the strong can remain free . . . only the strong can keep the peace'

It is further the cause of Republicanism to remind ourselves, and the world, that only the strong can remain free, that only the strong can keep the peace . . .

The Republican cause demands that we brand communism . . . as the only significant disturber of the peace, and we must make clear that until its goals of conquest are absolutely renounced . . . communism and the governments it now controls are enemies of every man on earth who is or wants to be free . . .

I believe that we must look beyond the defence of freedom today to its extension tomorrow . . . I suggest that all thoughtful men must contemplate the flowering of an Atlantic civilization, the whole world of Europe unified and free, trading openly across its borders, communicating openly across the world . . .

I can see a day when all the Americas, North and South, will be linked . . . in a rising tide of prosperity and interdependence . . .

And I pledge that the America I envision in the years ahead will extend its hand in health, in teaching and in cultivation, so that all new nations . . . will not wander down the dark alleys of tyranny or to the dead-end streets of collectivism. We do no man a service by hiding freedom's light under a bushel of mistaken humility . . .

But our example to the world must, like charity, begin at home . . . We must assure a society here which, while never abandoning the needy or forsaking the helpless, nurtures incentives and opportunity for the creative and the productive . . .

This nation . . . should again thrive upon the greatness of all those things which we, as individual citizens, can and should do. During the Republican years, this again will be . . . a nation where all who can will be self-reliant . . .

We Republicans seek a government that attends to its inherent responsibilities of maintaining a stable monetary and fiscal climate, encouraging a free and competitive economy and enforcing law and order. Thus do we seek inventiveness, diversity and creativity within a stable order, for we Republicans define government's role where needed at many, many levels, preferably through the one closest to the people involved. Our towns and our cities, then our counties, then our states, then our regional contacts – and only then, the national government. That is the ladder of liberty, built by decentralized power . . .

Balance, diversity, creativity – these are the elements of Republican equation . . . This is a party . . . for free men, not for blind followers, and not for conformists.

Back in 1858 Abraham Lincoln said this of the Republican party – and I quote him, because he probably could have said it during the last week or so: 'It was composed of strained, discordant, and even hostile elements' in 1858. Yet all of these elements agreed on one paramount objective: to arrest the progress of slavery, and place it in the course of ultimate extinction.

'Balance, diversity, creativity – these are the elements of Republican equation'

Today, as then, but more urgently and more broadly than then, the task of preserving and enlarging freedom at home and safeguarding it from the forces of tyranny abroad is great enough to challenge all our resources and to require all our strength . . .

I would remind you that extremism in the defence of liberty is no vice. And let me remind you also that moderation in the pursuit of justice is no virtue . . .

Our Republican cause is not to level out the world or make its people conform in computer-regimented sameness. Our Republican cause is to free our people and light the way for liberty throughout the world . . .

I accept your nomination . . . and you and I are going to fight for the goodness of our land.

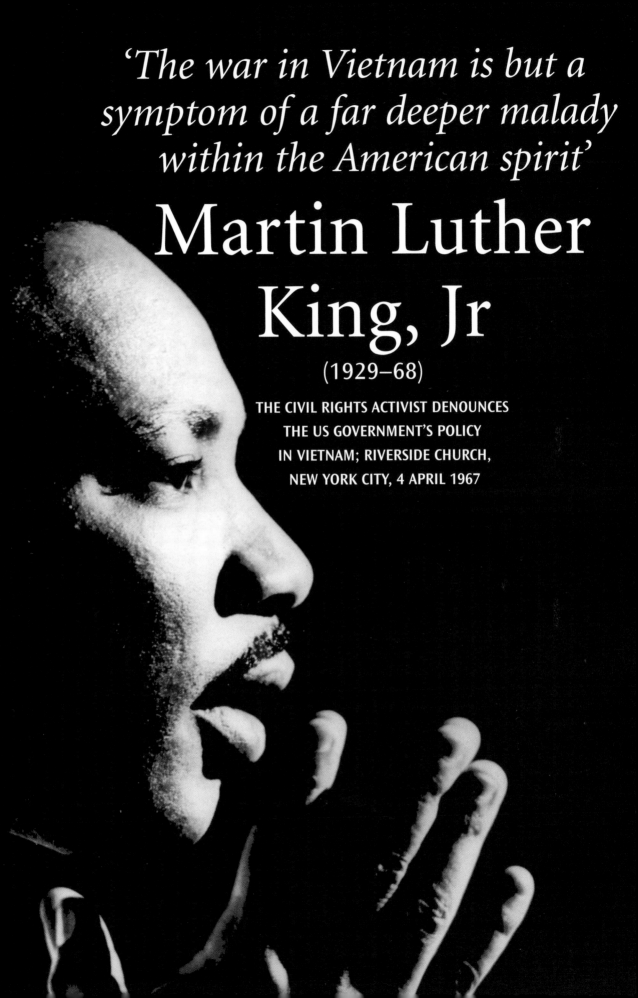

'The war in Vietnam is but a symptom of a far deeper malady within the American spirit'

Martin Luther King, Jr

(1929–68)

THE CIVIL RIGHTS ACTIVIST DENOUNCES
THE US GOVERNMENT'S POLICY
IN VIETNAM; RIVERSIDE CHURCH,
NEW YORK CITY, 4 APRIL 1967

King's leadership of the civil rights movement was based on the principle of non-violence, and in 1964 he had been awarded the Nobel Peace Prize. His effectiveness as a campaigner resulted in a comprehensive civil rights bill which, on becoming law in July 1964, outlawed segregation in public places and forbad racial discrimination in any enterprise which used federal money. The Voting Rights Act of 1965 outlawed discriminatory procedures in voter registration and the American South started to adapt to the new agenda.

This speech, entitled 'Beyond Vietnam', was King's response to a new turbulence which threatened to undermine recent progress in securing civil rights. President Johnson was overseeing an immense expansion in federal activity, and the 'Great Society' programme of legislation aimed at promoting opportunity for the hitherto marginalized, whether they were black or white. But the administration was also responsible for a spiralling defence budget as a result of the US military intervention in Vietnam, where America was the ally of the independent South, run by President Diem's dictatorial regime, and opposed to the equally sovereign North, which proclaimed itself to be a communist state. King protested that money spent on the Vietnam War would be better spent on 'programmes of social uplift', but his fears were also aroused by what was now happening in the American inner cities, where waves of violence undermined his aspiration for a racially integrated US achieved by pacifist means. On 12 August 1965 the Watts area of Los Angeles, a ghetto of 80,000 blacks, erupted in six days of race riots, and the summer of 1966 saw similar violence in other northern urban centres. Poor housing, inadequate education and high unemployment had created a black proletariat which considered itself excluded from American society. The new kind of activism which emerged from this milieu of the wretched and forgotten preached anti-white 'black power', and its most prominent representative was Malcolm X (1925–65), who rejected racial integration and urged instead black self-dependence.

King's commitment to democracy was now matched by his equally engaged awareness of a globalized instability. The US, he thought, was quite simply ending up on the wrong, and tyrannical, side of the argument in too many places across the world. His hostility to the US government's support for Latin American dictatorships and their claim to protect 'social stability' prefigured two decades of similar protests by King's compatriots. Criticism of big business sounded a new note in his rhetoric, but King remained the committed preacher – a Christian clinician diagnosing that 'malady within the American spirit' of which the Vietnam War was but a symptom. In calling for a worldwide 'revolution of values' King spoke as both a Christian and an American. The gospel was universal since it transcended nationality and American democracy could, in its own way, also heal a broken world. Rooted in the principles of a democratic revolution, the US was uniquely qualified to proclaim those same values and apply them to contemporary effect in a global crusade against militarism, poverty and racism. Redeeming the world meant reclaiming America.

'The war in Vietnam is but a symptom of a far deeper malady
within the American spirit'

I sometimes marvel at those who ask me why I am speaking against the war. Could it be that they do not know that the Good News was meant for all men . . . ? Have they forgotten that my ministry is in obedience to the one who loved His enemies so fully that he died for them? . . .

I must be true to my conviction that I share with all men the calling to be a son of the living God. Beyond the calling of race or nation or creed is this vocation of sonship and brotherhood . . . We are called to speak for the weak, for the voiceless, for the victims of our nation . . .

The Vietnamese people proclaimed their own independence in 1945 . . . Even though they quoted the American Declaration of Independence in their own document of freedom, we refused to recognize them. Instead, we decided to support France in its reconquest of her former colony . . .

'We are called to speak for the weak, for the voiceless, for the victims of our nation'

For nine years we vigorously supported the French in their abortive effort to recolonize Vietnam . . . We encouraged them with our huge financial and military supplies to continue the war even after they had lost the will. After the French were defeated, there came the United States . . . and the peasants watched as we supported one of the most vicious modern dictators, our chosen man, President Diem . . .

All the while the people read our leaflets and received the regular promises of peace and democracy and land reform. Now they languish under our bombs . . . They watch as we poison their water, as we kill a million acres of their crops . . . They wander into hospitals with at least 20 casualties from American firepower for one Vietcong-inflicted injury . . .

We have destroyed their two most cherished institutions: the family and the village . . . Now there is little left to build on, save bitterness . . .

I am as deeply concerned about our own troops there as anything else. For it occurs to me that what we are submitting them to in Vietnam is not simply the brutalizing process that goes on in any war where armies face each other and seek to destroy. We are adding cynicism to the process of death, for they must know after a short period that none of the things we claim to be fighting for are really involved. Before long they . . . surely realize that we are on the side of the wealthy, and the secure, while we create a hell for the poor.

Somehow this madness must cease. We must stop now. I speak as a child of God and brother to the suffering poor of Vietnam . . . I speak for the poor of America who are paying the double price of smashed hopes at home, and death and corruption in

Vietnam. I speak as a citizen of the world, for the world as it stands aghast at the path we have taken . . . In order to atone for our sins and errors in Vietnam, we should take the initiative in bringing a halt to this tragic war.

'I speak as a citizen of the world . . . as it stands aghast at the path we have taken'

The war in Vietnam is but a symptom of a far deeper malady within the American spirit . . . During the past ten years we have seen emerge a pattern of suppression which has now justified the presence of US military advisers in Venezuela. This need to maintain social stability for our investment accounts for the counter-revolutionary action of American forces in Guatemala. It tells why American helicopters are being used against guerrillas in Cambodia and why American napalm and Green Beret forces have already been active against rebels in Peru . . .

I am convinced that if we are to get on the right side of the world revolution, we as a nation must undergo a radical revolution of values . . . True compassion is more than flinging a coin to a beggar. It comes to see that an edifice which produces beggars needs restructuring.

'If we are to get on the right side of the world revolution, we as a nation must undergo a radical revolution of values'

A true revolution of values . . . will look across the seas and see individual capitalists of the West investing huge sums in Asia, Africa and South America, only to take the profits out with no concern for the social betterment of the countries . . .

A nation that continues year after year to spend more money on military defence than on programmes of social uplift is approaching spiritual death . . .

There is nothing except a tragic death wish to prevent us from reordering our priorities, so that the pursuit of peace will take precedence over the pursuit of war. There is nothing to keep us from moulding a recalcitrant status quo with bruised hands until we have fashioned it into a brotherhood . . .

We must not engage in a negative anti-communism, but rather in a positive thrust for democracy, realizing that our greatest defence against communism is to take offensive action in behalf of justice . . .

These are revolutionary times. All over the globe men are revolting against old systems of exploitation and oppression, and out of the wounds of a frail world new systems of justice and equality are being born. The shirtless and barefoot people of the land are rising up as never before. The people who sat in darkness have seen a great light . . .

The Western nations that initiated so much of the revolutionary spirit of the modern world have now become the arch anti-revolutionaries. This has driven many to feel that only Marxism has a revolutionary spirit . . . Our only hope today lies in our ability to recapture the revolutionary spirit and go out into a sometimes hostile world declaring eternal hostility to poverty, racism and militarism . . .

> ## *'Out of the wounds of a frail world new systems of justice and equality are being born'*

A genuine revolution of values means in the final analysis that our loyalties must become ecumenical rather than sectional . . .

This call for a worldwide fellowship that lifts neighbourly concern beyond one's tribe, race, class and nation is in reality a call for an all-embracing and unconditional love for all mankind . . .

We can no longer afford to worship the god of hate or bow before the altar of retaliation . . .

We must find new ways to speak for peace in Vietnam and justice throughout the developing world, a world that borders on our doors. If we do not act, we shall surely be dragged down the long, dark and shameful corridors of time reserved for those who possess power without compassion, might without morality and strength without sight.

'*Socialism is an attitude of mind*'

Julius Nyerere

(1922–99)

THE PRESIDENT OF TANZANIA DISCUSSES SOCIALISM ON BEING AWARDED
AN HONORARY DEGREE BY THE UNIVERSITY OF CAIRO;
EGYPT, 10 APRIL 1967

'Socialism is an attitude of mind'

Throughout his period in office Julius Nyerere preached 'African socialism' – his idiosyncratic blend of rural values and left-wing intellectualism. He was known as *Mwalimu*, the Swahili for 'teacher', not just in his native Tanganyika but right across the African continent, and the didactic tone of this particular address typified Nyerere's speeches in general. The African countryside was, in his view, innately communal, since its characteristic social structure was supposed to be that of the *ujamaa*, or extended household. Tanganyika's rural population was therefore deemed to be naturally (albeit unselfconsciously) socialist – people who would adapt readily to their president's socio-economic experimentation.

In formulating his goals Nyerere was much influenced by British socialism's Fabian tradition – a school of thought with a high view of government and a progressivist zeal for organizing other people's lives. Nyerere's personal life was austere and his Catholic spirituality was reflected in his habit of regular fasting and daily attendance at mass. The sincerity of his political idealism and evident incorruptibility won him a vast and devoted personal following, and for many he was the face of Africa itself in its immediate postcolonial period. He won plaudits for his moderation when leading the movement for Tanganyika's self-determination, and an orderly transfer of power from the British colonial administration secured his installation as leader of a one-party state.

Nyerere's speech idealizes a traditional past when African workers owned their own tools or 'means of production' and travelled independently to markets where they could sell or

JULIUS NYERERE (1922–99)

1937 Enters Tabora Government School, and subsequently attends Makerere University, Uganda.

1949 Wins scholarship to Edinburgh University; graduates (1952) in economics and history, and teaches subsequently in Dar es Salaam.

1953 President of Tanganyika African Association, a group of public sector workers, which becomes in 1954 the Tanganyika African National Union, a body working for independence.

1958 Enters Colonial Legislative Council and elected (1960) chief minister.

1961 Tanganyika gains independence; becomes country's first prime minister.

1962 President of Tanganyika, which is now a republic.

1964 Zanzibar unites with Tanganyika to form Tanzania.

Feb 1967 Arusha Declaration.

1978 Declares war on Uganda, whose ruler Idi Amin is toppled in 1979.

1985 Resigns presidency amid economic chaos; successors adopt free-market policies.

1992 Tanzania becomes a multi-party democracy.

barter produce – their appropriate means of 'distribution and exchange'. Introduction of money had destroyed this primitive arcadia, and its particular economic structure could not be re-established. But communal ownership of the means of production, distribution and exchange would nonetheless recapture the cooperative values associated with this imagined past. Nyerere acknowledges that the effectiveness of such a system presupposes the existence of an incorruptible political and administrative elite, an insight which had not prevented him from issuing the Arusha Declaration and its embrace of an *ujamaa*-based socialism just months earlier. The document pledged his government to the 'villagization' of the rural economy: a previously scattered population farming small holdings would be congregated in village units designed to be large enough to provide communal services and increase production levels. Widespread resentment was aroused by this collectivization of farming when it was enforced in the mid-1970s and the programme was abandoned after a few years. The malign effects, however, were long-lived and the renamed Tanzania, having been a massive exporter of agricultural produce, became a net importer experiencing acute levels of poverty. Socialism in its *ujamaa* guise aimed to secure national self-sufficiency in all areas of the economy, and its application through the Basic Industrial Strategy led to the nationalization of banks and key industries. But there was little that was 'self-sufficient' about a country burdened by a massive national debt, plagued by balance of payments crises and dependent on International Monetary Fund loans. Nyerere's words had turned to dust.

'Over time there have been many definitions of socialism . . . Unfortunately, however, there has grown up what I can only call a 'theology of socialism'. People argue – sometimes quite violently – about what is the true doctrine . . . I think that this idea that there is one 'pure socialism', for which the recipe is already known, is an insult to human intelligence. It seems to me that man has yet to solve the problem of living in society, and that each of us may have something to contribute to the problems it involves. We should recognize that there are books on socialism which can illuminate the problems, and books which chart a way forward from a particular point. But that is all . . .

'This idea that there is one "pure socialism", for which the recipe is already known, is an insult to human intelligence'

Yet I am not saying that socialism is a vague concept . . . For socialism the basic purpose is the well-being of the people and the basic assumption is an acceptance of human equality . . . The human equality before God which is the basis of all the great religions of the world is also the basis of the political philosophy of socialism. Yet socialism is not

Utopian . . . It is a recognition that some human beings are physically strong and others weak, that some are intellectually able whilst others are rather dull, that some are skilful in the use of their hands whilst others are clumsy. It involves, too, a recognition that every person has both a selfish and a social instinct, which are often in conflict. Socialist doctrine then demands the deliberate organization of society in such a manner that it is impossible – or at least very difficult – for individual desires to be pursued at the cost of other people . . .

'Socialism is not Utopian'

For a socialist state these requirements have both a negative and a positive aspect. Men must be prevented from exploiting each other. And at the same time institutions and organizations must be such that man's needs and progress can be cooperatively secured. There are two paths through which exploitation has been historically secured and which must therefore be blocked. The first was the use of naked force. Originally through physical strength, and then through a monopoly of weapons of force, men imposed their will upon others . . . The gradual growth of law, and the principle of equality before the law, ease the severity of oppression until the people are in a position to take control of their own destiny.

The second major means of exploitation has been through private property . . . The man whose means of living are controlled by another must serve the interests of this other regardless of his own desires or his own needs . . .

If a society is to be made up of equal citizens, then each man must control his own means of production. The farmer must own his own tools – his hoe or his plough. The carpenter must have his own saw and not be dependent upon the whims of another for its use. The tools of production must be under the control of the individual or group which depends upon them for life.

In African traditional life this was the normal routine . . . But there can be no going back to this system – which has now suffered considerably from the effects of a money economy . . .

'The farmer must own his own tools – his hoe or his plough'

In those areas of production where individual ownership of tools is impractical we are therefore forced to the conclusion that group ownership of the means of production is the only way in which the exploitation of man by man can be prevented. This communal ownership can be through the state, which represents every citizen, or through some other institution which is controlled by those involved – such as, for example, a cooperative or a local authority.

The same thing applies to the question of distribution and exchange. In small peasant societies it is possible for each grower or each producer to bring his goods to a central place and bargain . . . But the increasing specialization of production requires more sophisticated techniques. And once again, a private individual can get into a position where he controls the well-being of another. He can do this by his charges for transport, by his commission on sales, or by exploiting a monopoly position. Communal ownership of the means of distribution and communal enterprise in the act of bargaining can eliminate this kind of exploitation.

Yet although the facts of modern technology provide the final justification for the communal ownership of the means of production and exchange, it is not always and everywhere appropriate . . . It is possible, as we have found out in Tanzania, for farmers to be exploited even by their own cooperative and their own state if the machinery is not correct, or if the managers and workers are inefficient or dishonest . . .

For it is not good enough just to deprive people of the incentives of selfishness. Development requires that these should be replaced by effective social incentives . . . Public ownership may not necessarily and always be the correct answer for socialists at a particular time . . . A decision should depend on the circumstances and the prevailing attitudes – that is, on the success of socialist political education . . .

'It is not good enough just to deprive people of the incentives of selfishness'

In 1962 I said that socialism is an attitude of mind. I still believe this to be true . . . Without the correct attitudes, institutions can be subverted from their true purpose . . . There must be, among the leadership, a desire and determination to serve alongside of, and in complete identification with, the masses.

If the people are not honestly served by those to whom they have entrusted responsibility, then corruption can negate all their efforts and make them abandon their socialist ideas . . .

This is a technological age, and many decisions cannot be taken directly by the masses. Tremendous responsibilities therefore rest upon those of us who have had the privilege of higher education . . . Our function is to serve, to guide the masses through the complexities of modern technology – to propose, to explain and to persuade . . . And unless we who have the power – whether it be political or technical – remain at one with the masses, then we cannot serve them.

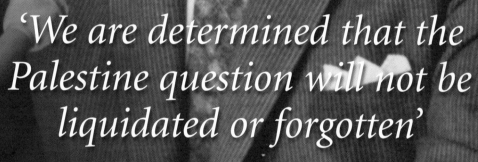

'*We are determined that the Palestine question will not be liquidated or forgotten*'

Gamal Abdel Nasser

(1918–70)

THE PRESIDENT OF EGYPT ADDRESSES
ARAB TRADE UNIONISTS; 26 MAY 1967

These speeches are among Nasser's many declamations while preparing for war in the spring of 1967. He was speaking not just as Egypt's president but also as the advocate of pan-Arabism – the belief that the Middle East's Arab states should strive for unity.

'The 1961 secession' refers to Syria's decision to withdraw from the United Arab Republic, an unsatisfactory three-year experiment conjoining Egypt with Syria and scant proof of a 'union . . . achieved'. Over a decade had passed since the Suez episode enhanced Nasser's prestige and he was now under pressure to take military action to redress Palestinian grievances. The UN Emergency Force's presence in the Sinai during that period had stopped any remilitarization of the peninsula by either Israel or Egypt. On 16 May 1967 Nasser ordered UNEF's immediate withdrawal and Egyptian forces moved across the Sinai to take up positions on Israel's border. On 23 May he closed the Straits of Tiran to Israeli shipping, thereby blocking Israel's southern port of Eilat and the country's access to the Indian Ocean.

Nasser speaks here at the height of his influence. Muammar al-Gaddafi of Libya and Ahmed Ben Bella of Algeria were among the Arab leaders who emulated him. He ran Egypt through an efficient police and security apparatus, and in the early 1960s he nationalized most of the country's industrial, commercial and financial sectors. Though he disliked communism, he liked Soviet aid, and the USSR helped pay for the Aswan High Dam which boosted Egypt's electricity supplies. In these speeches he stirs pan-Arab sentiment to

GAMAL ABDEL NASSER (1918–70)

1939 Graduates from Egyptian Military Academy, Cairo.

1948–9 Serves in the Arab–Israeli War, and subsequently becomes an instructor at Cairo's Military Academy.

1949 Forms coordinating committee of the Free Officers Movement (FOM) and in 1950 becomes its head.

23 July 1952 The FOM seizes control of the Egyptian government, subsequently forming the Egyptian Revolutionary Command Council.

1954 Becomes president of Egypt.

1956–7 The Suez Crisis raises his authority.

1962 Promotes the Arab nationalist coup d'état establishing the Yemen Arab Republic.

1967 Egypt loses the Sinai as a result of the Six Day War (5–10 June).

1969 Dismisses more than one hundred judges.

1970 An estimated five million mourners attend his funeral in Cairo.

characteristic effect with his portrayal of an Arab civilization whose historic glories have been revived magnificently. Medieval crusaders are compared to modern Westerners contemptuous of Arab dignity. Injustice is about to be punished.

Jordan and Syria would wage war as Egypt's allies. Iraq, Saudi Arabia, Sudan, Tunisia, Morocco and Algeria committed troops and equipment. This was as pan-Arab as it could get. Israel responded to the threat pre-emptively and in the Six Day War (5–10 June 1967) smashed its enemies' offensive capacity in an awesome display of strategic power. The first wave of strikes on Egypt's airfields destroyed some 300 of her 450 combat aircraft, all Soviet-built and up to date. Within two days total losses of enemy aircraft amounted to 416, and the air forces of Jordan, Syria and Iraq played no further role in hostilities. Israel gained the River Jordan's West Bank – including East Jerusalem – the Golan Heights, the Gaza Strip and the entire Sinai Peninsula. Over half a million West Bank Palestinians now lived on Israeli land, and another 300,000 of them had fled to Jordan. Jordan and Egypt would eventually withdraw their claim to, respectively, the West Bank and Gaza. The Sinai was returned to Egypt in 1978 and Israel withdrew from Gaza in 2005.

The war shattered pan-Arabism and its largely secularist impulses would be replaced by those of Islamist fundamentalism. On 9 June 1967 Nasser tried to resign. Popular street protests persuaded him to stay but he never regained the self-confidence expressed in these grandiloquent phrases.

You, the Arab workers' federation, represent the biggest force in the Arab world. We can achieve much by Arab action, which is a main part of our battle. Despair has never found its way into Arab hearts and never will. What we see today in the masses of the Arab peoples everywhere is their desire to fight. The Arab people want to regain the rights of the people of Palestine.

We sustained heavy losses in 1956. Later, union was achieved. The 1961 secession occurred when we had barely begun to stand firmly on our feet. We were waiting for the day when we would be confident of being able to adopt strong measures if we were to enter the battle with Israel. Recently we felt that we could triumph. On this basis, we decided to take steps.

'The Arab people want to regain the rights of the people of Palestine'

Many people blamed us for the presence of the UN Emergency Force. Should we have listened to them, or rather built and trained our army while UNEF still existed? Once we were fully prepared, we could ask UNEF to leave. And this is what actually happened.

With regard to military plans, there is complete coordination of military action between us and Syria. We will operate as one army fighting a single battle for the sake of a common objective – the objective of the Arab nation.

'The problem today is not just Israel, but also those behind it'

The problem today is not just Israel, but also those behind it. If Israel embarks on an aggression against Syria and Egypt, the battle against Israel will be a general one and not confined to one spot on the Syrian or Egyptian borders. Our basic objective will be to destroy Israel. I probably could not have said such things five or even three years ago. Today I say such things because I am confident. I know what we have here in Egypt and what Syria has. I also know that Iraq has sent its troops to Syria; Algeria will send troops; Kuwait also will send troops. This is Arab power. This is the true resurrection of the Arab nation.

We are not states without status. Our states have thousands of years of civilization behind them – 7000 years of civilization. We shall not relinquish our rights. We want the front to become one united front around Israel. We will not relinquish the rights of the people of Palestine.

'This is the true resurrection of the Arab nation'

During the crusaders' occupation, the Arabs waited 70 years before a suitable opportunity arose and they drove away the crusaders. Some people commented that Abdel Nasser said we should shelve the Palestinian question for 70 years, but I say that as a people with an ancient civilization, as an Arab people, we are determined that the Palestine question will not be liquidated or forgotten. The whole question is the proper time to achieve our aims. We are preparing ourselves constantly. You are the hope of the Arab nation and its vanguard. As workers, you are actually building the Arab nation. The quicker we build, the quicker we will be able to achieve our aim.

'We are now ready to deal with the entire Palestine question'

THE EGYPTIAN PRESIDENT ADDRESSES MEMBERS OF THE EGYPTIAN NATIONAL ASSEMBLY; 29 MAY 1967

The circumstances through which we are now passing are difficult because we are not only confronting Israel but also the West, which created Israel and despised us Arabs and which ignored us before and since 1948. They had no regard whatsoever for our feelings, our hopes in life, our rights. The Arab nation was unable to check the West's course.

Then came the events of 1956 – the Suez battle. When we rose to demand our rights, Britain, France and Israel opposed us. We resisted, however, and proclaimed that we would fight to the last drop of our blood. God gave us success and God's victory was great.

'We would fight to the last drop of our blood'

Subsequently we were able to rise and build. Now, 11 years after 1956, we are restoring things to what they were in 1956. This is from the material aspect. In my opinion this material aspect is only a small part, whereas the spiritual aspect is the great side of the issue. The spiritual aspect involves the renaissance of the Arab nation, the revival of the Palestine question, and the restoration of confidence to every Arab and to every Palestinian. God will surely help us and urge us to restore the situation to what it was in 1948.

'The spiritual aspect involves the renaissance of the Arab nation'

Israel used to boast a great deal, and the Western powers, headed by the United States and Britain, used to consider us of no value. But now that the time has come, we must be ready for triumph and not for a recurrence of the 1948 comedies. Preparations have already been made. Now we are ready for the confrontation. We are now ready to deal with the entire Palestine question. We demand the full rights of the Palestinian people. Arabs throughout the Arab world are demanding these rights.

'The time has come, we must be ready for triumph'

The United States and Britain give no consideration to the entire Arab nation. Why? Because we have made them believe that we cannot distinguish between friend and foe. We must make them know that we know who our foes are and who our friends are and treat them accordingly. I wish to tell you today that the Soviet Union is a friendly power and stands by us as a friend. In all our dealings with the Soviet Union – and I have been dealing with the USSR since 1955 – it has not made a single request of us. The USSR has never interfered with our policy or internal affairs. This is the USSR as we have always known it. Last year we asked for wheat and they sent it to us. When I asked for all kinds of arms, they gave them to us. The war minister yesterday handed me a message from the Soviet premier Kosygin saying that the USSR supported us in this battle and would not allow any power to intervene until matters were restored to what they were in 1956.

Brothers, we will work for world peace with all the power at our disposal, but we will also hold tenaciously to our rights with all the power at our disposal.

'*North Vietnam cannot defeat or humiliate the United States. Only Americans can do that*'

Richard Nixon
(1913–94)

THE US PRESIDENT SIGNALS A CHANGE OF COURSE IN VIETNAM;
TELEVISED ADDRESS TO THE AMERICAN PEOPLE,
3 NOVEMBER 1969

Duurng his presidential campaign Richard Nixon pledged that he would, if elected, end the Vietnam War, and the first reductions in US troop levels in South Vietnam were announced in June 1969. US foreign policy under Nixon abandoned the 'domino theory' which maintained that a North Vietnamese victory would inevitably lead to communist governments throughout southeast Asia. But he had also promised 'peace with honour', by which he meant the maintenance of US credibility as a superpower. This typically skilful address therefore deploys some of the vigorous anti-communist rhetoric which had marked Nixon's earlier career. Menacing states devoted to 'world conquest' would seek to profit from the US's humiliation were it to be defeated in South Vietnam, and America's 'national destiny' involved 'free-world leadership'.

The appeal to the 'silent majority' marked the latest evolution of a continuous Nixon theme: the contrast between a noisy 'liberal elite' and those hard-working, undemonstrative Americans who supplied the nation with its enduring identity. Nonetheless, few American citizens were taken in by the policy of Vietnamization and its application of the 'Nixon Doctrine'. Their country was retreating and the South Vietnamese army, however well trained by the departing ally and despite its liberal endowment with US military hardware, was obviously incapable of withstanding an all-out assault by the combined forces of the People's Army of Vietnam (PAVN) and the National Front for the Liberation of South Vietnam (the Vietcong guerrillas).

Two-thirds of the original US combat force of just over half a million had left South Vietnam by the end of 1971. But the need to maintain both the US's military authority and its diplomatic credibility meant that the administration had to mask the truth that

RICHARD NIXON (1913-94)

1937 Admitted to the US bar and practises law in California.

1946 Elected to US House of Representatives.

1948 As member of the House Un-American Activities Committee, exposes Alger Hiss, a State Department official, as a Soviet spy.

1950 Elected to US Senate.

1952 Elected vice president of the US.

1960 Becomes the Republican Party's nominee for the presidency; narrowly defeated by the Democratic candidate John F. Kennedy.

1962 Fails to be elected governor of California, informs journalists: 'You won't have Nixon to kick around anymore.'

1968 Elected president of the US.

9 August 1974 Resigns presidency.

'North Vietnam cannot defeat or humiliate the United States.
Only Americans can do that'

Vietnamization really meant withdrawal. Nixon therefore seized the opportunity to extend the war to neighbouring Cambodia, which had been protected previously by its neutrality. By 1969 Prince Norodom Sihanouk, the country's ruler, was declaring that he wanted closer US relations, and General Lon Nol, who deposed him in March 1970, was pro-American. US and South Vietnamese forces were therefore able to attack PAVN and Vietcong troops encamped on Cambodia's eastern border with Vietnam. Operation Menu was conducted over 14 months during 1969–70, but few Americans listening to Nixon's address would have known of this massive bombing campaign. The president had ignored the need for Congressional approval and the operation's covert nature made it the first of his subversions of the US constitution.

Cambodia's bombing nonetheless did the trick for Nixon since it amounted to a shield behind which Vietnamization could proceed. Yet for the president that disengagement was but one element in a wider picture: the pursuit of détente, or the easing of tension, with the USSR and China. The Cambodian bombing was intended to show these communist states that America would be negotiating with them from a position of continued strength. Words, though, as well as deeds, still mattered in the conduct of such diplomacy and this speech's projection of US power was intended to be heard in Moscow and Beijing as well as in America.

‘

Fifteen years ago North Vietnam, with the logistical support of communist China and the Soviet Union, launched a campaign to impose a communist government on South Vietnam by instigating and supporting a revolution.

In response to the request of the government of South Vietnam, President Eisenhower sent economic aid and military equipment . . . Seven years ago, President Kennedy sent 16,000 military personnel to Vietnam as combat advisers. Four years ago President Johnson sent American combat forces to South Vietnam.

Now, many believe that President Johnson's decision was wrong. And many others – I among them – have been strongly critical of the way the war has been conducted.

But the question facing us today is: Now that we are in the war, what is the best way to end it? . . .

For the South Vietnamese, our precipitate withdrawal would inevitably allow the communists to repeat the massacres which followed their takeover in the North 15 years before . . .

'Now that we are in the war, what is the
best way to end it?'

For the United States, this first defeat in our nation's history would result in a collapse of confidence in American leadership, not only in Asia but throughout the world . . .

Our defeat and humiliation in South Vietnam without question would promote recklessness in the councils of those great powers who have not yet abandoned their goals of world conquest. This would spark violence wherever our commitments help maintain the peace – in the Middle East, in Berlin, eventually even in the western hemisphere . . .

> *'This first defeat in our nation's history*
> *would result in a collapse*
> *of confidence in*
> *American leadership'*

For these reasons, I rejected the recommendation that I should end the war by immediately withdrawing all our forces. I chose instead to change American policy on both the negotiating front and battlefront . . .

– We have offered the complete withdrawal of all outside forces within one year.

– We have proposed a ceasefire under international supervision.

– We have offered free elections under international supervision with the communists participating in the organization and conduct of the elections . . .

Hanoi has refused even to discuss our proposals. They demand . . . that we withdraw all American forces immediately and unconditionally and that we overthrow the government of South Vietnam as we leave . . .

It has become clear that the obstacle in negotiating an end to the war . . . is the other side's absolute refusal to show the least willingness to join us in seeking a just peace . . .

At the time we launched our search for peace I recognized we might not succeed in bringing an end to the war through negotiation. I therefore put into effect another plan which will bring the war to an end regardless of what happens on the negotiating front.

It is in line with a major shift in US foreign policy which . . . has been described as the Nixon Doctrine . . .

> *'We Americans are a do-it-yourself people.*
> *We are an impatient people'*

'North Vietnam cannot defeat or humiliate the United States.
Only Americans can do that'

We Americans are a do-it-yourself people. We are an impatient people. Instead of teaching someone else to do a job, we like to do it ourselves. And this trait has been carried over into our foreign policy.

In Korea and again in Vietnam, the United States furnished most of the money, most of the arms and most of the men to help the people of those countries defend their freedom against communist aggression . . .

'In this administration we are Vietnamizing the search for peace'

I laid down three principles as guidelines for future American policy towards Asia:

– First, the United States will keep all of its treaty commitments.

– Second, we shall provide a shield if a nuclear power threatens the freedom of a nation allied with us or of a nation whose survival we consider vital to our security.

– Third, in cases involving other types of aggression, we shall furnish military and economic assistance when requested in accordance with our treaty commitments. But we shall look to the nation directly threatened to assume the primary responsibility of providing the manpower for its defence . . .

In the previous administration, we Americanized the war in Vietnam. In this administration we are Vietnamizing the search for peace . . . Under the new orders, the primary mission of our troops is to enable the South Vietnamese forces to assume the full responsibility for the security of South Vietnam . . .

We have adopted a plan . . . for the complete withdrawal of all US combat ground forces, and their replacement by South Vietnamese forces . . . As South Vietnamese forces become stronger, the rate of American withdrawal can become greater . . .

In speaking of the consequences of a precipitate withdrawal, I mentioned that our allies would lose confidence in America.

Far more dangerous, we would lose confidence in ourselves. Oh, the immediate reaction would be a sense of relief that our men were coming home. But as we saw the consequences of what we had done, inevitable remorse and divisive recrimination would scar our spirit as a people . . .

I know it may not be fashionable to speak of patriotism or national destiny these days. But I feel it is appropriate to do so on this occasion.

Two hundred years ago this nation was weak and poor . . . Today we have become the strongest and richest nation in the world . . . Any hope the world has for the survival of peace and freedom will be determined by whether the American people have the courage to meet the challenge of free-world leadership . . .

And so tonight – to you, the great silent majority of my fellow Americans – I ask for your support . . .

> *'To you, the great silent majority of my fellow Americans – I ask for your support'*

Let us be united for peace. Let us also be united against defeat. Because let us understand: North Vietnam cannot defeat or humiliate the United States. Only Americans can do that.

Fifty years ago, in this room and at this very desk, President Woodrow Wilson . . . said: 'This is the war to end war.' His dream for peace after World War I was shattered on the hard realities of great power politics and Woodrow Wilson died a broken man.

Tonight I do not tell you that the war in Vietnam is the war to end wars. But I do say this: I have initiated a plan which will end this war in a way that will bring us closer to that great goal to which Woodrow Wilson and every American president in our history has been dedicated – the goal of a just and lasting peace.

'*Mistakes, yes. But for
personal gain, never*'

Richard Nixon

(1913–94)

THE DISGRACED PRESIDENT MAKES HIS FAREWELL SPEECH TO WHITE HOUSE STAFF;
WASHINGTON, 9 AUGUST 1974

I n November 1972 Richard Nixon was re-elected president in a landslide which saw him carry 49 of the Union's 50 states and gain over 60 per cent of the popular vote. His record as one of the great reforming presidents in domestic and foreign affairs helps explain that victory. Nixon ended the Vietnam War, and his policies, based on realism rather than ideology, led to the establishment of US diplomatic relations with China. The treaty agreed between the US and the USSR in May 1972 on the limitation of anti-ballistic missile systems was a milestone in the history of détente. Many federal agencies, such as those regulating environmental protection and enforcing anti-drugs legislation, were established during the Nixon presidency, a period which marks a high point in the history of US governmental activism. Desegregation in the public schools of the American South became rapid and irreversible, and in February 1974 Nixon introduced a measure which would have forced employers to buy health insurance for their employees. But the Nixon White House also became synonymous with a paranoid style of government whose suspicions, resentments and illegalities were directly attributable to the president's own personality and fears.

At 11.35 a.m. on the day he delivered this speech Nixon formally resigned the presidency by signing a letter addressed to Secretary of State Henry Kissinger. Facing impeachment by the House of Representatives and almost certain conviction by the Senate, he had been forced out of office by the evidence of his complicity in the attempt to conceal his officials' involvement in the Watergate scandal. On 17 June 1972 five burglars were arrested after breaking into the headquarters of the Democratic Party's National Committee at the Watergate Hotel in Washington DC. Their links with the Committee to Re-elect the President (CREEP), a White House funding organization, led to Nixon being named an 'unindicted co-conspirator' by the grand jury investigating the affair. Watergate, however, meant more than just a single, bungled burglary since its investigation revealed an even wider pattern of 'dirty tricks', many of which related to Nixon's dislike of the media. Concerned about the leaking of governmental information to the press, from 1969 onwards he had been authorizing the illegal tapping of the phones of journalists and of administration officials. Nixon's legacy included a widespread loss of belief among Americans in the probity of US government but, following his successor's grant of an official pardon, criminal charges could not be brought against him.

This speech shows many of Nixon's finer qualities: personal resilience, an easy command of his audience and the unaffected eloquence of a born orator. The affecting description of his childhood and of his parents' struggles in life reveal the depths to his character – as well as explaining in part the edge to his personality. Formed by early adversity, Nixon always regarded himself as a loner, and even as president he had behaved like an outsider whose aims had to be achieved by stealth. That combative style had been both the making and the unmaking of the most complex president in American history.

'Mistakes, yes. But for personal gain, never'

You are here to say goodbye to us, and we don't have a good word for it in English. The best is *au revoir*. We will see you again . . . I ask all of you . . . to serve our next president as you have served me and previous presidents – because many of you have been here for many years – with devotion and dedication, because this office, great as it is, can only be as great as the men and women who work for and with the president.

This house, for example, I was thinking of it as we walked down this hall, and I was comparing it to some of the great houses of the world that I have been in. This isn't the biggest house . . . This isn't the finest house. Many in Europe, particularly, and in China, Asia, have paintings of great value, things that we just don't have here, and probably will never have until we are 1000 years old or older.

> *'This office, great as it is, can only be as great as the men and women who work for and with the president'*

But this is the best house. It is the best house because it has something far more important than numbers of people who serve, far more important than numbers of rooms or how big it is, far more important than numbers of magnificent pieces of art. This house has a great heart, and that heart comes from those who serve . . .

Sure we have done some things wrong in this administration, and the top man always takes the responsibility, and I have never ducked it. But I want to say one thing: we can be proud of it – five and a half years. No man or woman came into this administration and left it with more of this world's goods than when he came in . . . Mistakes, yes. But for personal gain, never . . .

You are getting something . . . in government service that is far more important than money. It is a cause bigger than yourself. It is the cause of making this the greatest nation in the world, the leader of the world, because without our leadership the world will know nothing but war, possible starvation, or worse, in the years ahead. With our leadership it will know peace, it will know plenty . . .

You know, people often come in and say, ' What will I tell my kids?' They look at government and say it is sort of a rugged life, and they see the mistakes that are made. They get the impression that everybody is here for the purpose of feathering his nest. That is why I made this earlier point – not in this administration, not one single man or woman.

I remembered my old man. I think that they would have called him sort of a little man, common man. He didn't consider himself that way. You know what he was? He was a streetcar motorman first, and then he was a farmer, and then he had a lemon ranch. It was the poorest lemon ranch in California, I can assure you. He sold it before they found oil on it. And then he was a grocer. But he was a great man because he did his job, and every job counts up to the hilt, regardless of what happens.

Nobody will ever write a book, probably, about my mother. Well, I guess all of you would say this about your mother – my mother was a saint. And I think of her, two boys dying to tuberculosis, nursing four others in order that she could take care of my older brother for three years in Arizona, and seeing each of them die, and when they died, it was like one of her own. Yes, she will have no books written about her. But she was a saint.

Now, however, we look to the future. I had a little quote in the speech last night from T.R. [Theodore Roosevelt]. As you know, I kind of like to read books. I am not educated, but I do read books [laughter] and the T.R. quote was a pretty good one. Here is another one I found as I was reading, my last night in the White House . . . He was a young lawyer in New York. He had married a beautiful girl . . . and then suddenly she died, and this is what he wrote. This was in his diary:

> She was beautiful in face and lovelier still in spirit . . . When she had just become a mother, when her life seemed to be just begun and when the years seemed so bright before her, then by a strange and terrible fate death came to her. And when my heart's dearest died, the light went from my life forever.

That was T.R. in his twenties. He thought the light had gone from his life forever – but he went on. And he not only became president but, as an ex-president, he served his country always in the arena, tempestuous, strong, sometimes wrong, sometimes right, but he was a man.

And as I leave, let me say, that is an example all of us should remember. We think sometimes when things happen that don't go the right way; we think that when you don't pass the bar exam the first time – I happened to, but I was just lucky; I mean my writing was so poor that the bar examiner said, 'We have just got to let the guy through.' [Laughter] We think that when someone dear to us dies, we think that when we lose an election, we think that when we suffer defeat, that all is ended. We think, as T.R. said, that the light had left his life forever.

Not true. It is only a beginning always. The young must know it; the old must know it. It must always sustain us because the greatness comes . . . when you take some knocks, some disappointments, when sadness comes, because only if you have been in the deepest valley can you ever know how magnificent it is to be at the highest mountain.

And so, we leave with high hopes, in good spirits and with deep humility, and with very much gratefulness in our hearts. I can only say to each and every one of you, we come from many faiths, we pray perhaps to different gods, but really the same God in a sense . . . I want to say . . . always you will be in our hearts and you will be in our prayers.

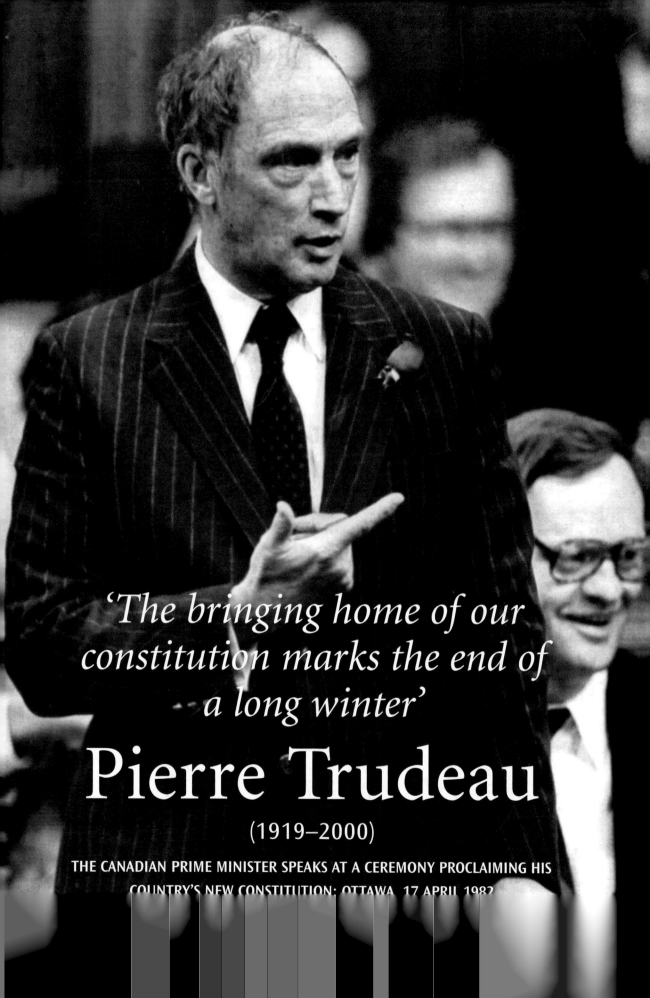

'The bringing home of our constitution marks the end of a long winter'

Pierre Trudeau

(1919–2000)

THE CANADIAN PRIME MINISTER SPEAKS AT A CEREMONY PROCLAIMING HIS
COUNTRY'S NEW CONSTITUTION: OTTAWA, 17 APRIL 1982

Pierre Trudeau's intellectual agility and personal flair dominated late 20th-century Canadian history and helped to ensure the country's survival as a federal state. The 1982 Constitution Act is his most significant achievement, and the speech Trudeau delivered at its formal proclamation illustrates the clarity of his legal thought and an equally characteristic progressivism. Although Canada already had a bill of rights (1960), the incorporation of a 'Charter of Rights and Freedoms' in the new measure provided a more precise definition of individual freedoms and strengthened the judges' role in the interpretation and enforcement of its provisions. Taken as a whole, Trudeau's legislative package aimed at the entrenchment of a collective Canadian identity, and he eventually persuaded nine out of the ten provincial premiers to support the Canada Act, though their formal consent was not necessary. The government of Quebec never formally approved the measure.

Trudeau was a Quebecer formed by the province's francophone traditions at a time when the predominant milieu was one of conservative-minded clericalism. A Jesuit education at Montreal's Collège Jean-de-Brébeuf trained him in dialectical sharpness and encouraged his early leanings towards Quebec nationalism. He took a detached view of the Second World War in the course of which he was a reluctant conscript and never served overseas. During the postwar period, however, he became increasingly committed to the cause of individual rights and formed the view that their protection and advancement within Canada required the survival and strengthening of the country's federal government. Trudeau's early years as premier saw the passage of measures decriminalizing homosexuality, legalizing abortion and controlling gun ownership. The country became officially bilingual and the provision

PIERRE TRUDEAU (1919–2000)

1943 Graduates from Montreal University.

1946–7 Studies at École des Sciences Politiques, Paris.

1961–5 Associate Professor of Law, Montreal University.

1965 Joins Liberal Party; elected to the Canadian parliament.

1967 Appointed minister of justice.

1968 Becomes prime minister, having been elected Liberal Party leader, and wins subsequent (25 June) general election.

1972 Forms a minority government supported by the left-wing New Democratic Party.

1974 Re-elected prime minister; forms majority government.

1979 Liberal government defeated by Progressive Conservatives, whose government loses (Dec) a parliamentary motion of no confidence.

Feb 1980 Wins general election.

June 1984 Resigns premiership.

of federal services in both French and English sought to secure the two communities' rapprochement. The 'October Crisis' of 1970 tested Trudeau's leadership when the *Front de libération du Québec* embarked on a terrorist campaign, and his application of the War Measures Act – including arrest and detention without trial – confirmed his stature as a resolute leader. Quebec nationalism lost its extremist tinge but nonetheless retained its political edge.

Economic crisis in the 1970s threatened Trudeau's balancing act as he tried to reconcile the country's provinces to each other and to win support for the expansion of the federal government's welfare programmes. He introduced wage and price controls in 1975, and the National Energy Programme (1980) attempted to reduce spiralling rates of inflation and of interest by using Petro-Canada, a publicly owned company, to regulate the country's oil industry. The programme's promotion of lower prices was unpopular in oil-producing western Canada and, shorn of its commodity profits, the region developed its own separatist ambitions. Trudeau's personal and political unpopularity meant that not a single Liberal candidate was elected west of Manitoba in the 1980 election, though in Quebec a referendum of that year saw 60 per cent of those voting reject independence for the province. Québécois hostility to the Canada Act kept the sovereignty issue alive, however, and in the 1995 referendum 49.4 per cent voted for independence as opposed to 50.6 per cent who opted for the status quo. Protected in their rights by the Canada Act, Quebec's aboriginal peoples had voted overwhelmingly to endorse the union which had become their Canadian home.

Today, at long last, Canada is acquiring full and complete national sovereignty. The constitution of Canada has come home. The most fundamental law of the land will now be capable of being amended in Canada, without any further recourse to the parliament of the United Kingdom . . .

For more than half a century, Canadians have resembled young adults who leave home to build a life of their own, but are not quite confident enough to take along all their belongings. We became an independent country for all practical purposes in 1931, with the passage of the Statute of Westminster. But by our own choice, because of our inability to agree upon an amending formula at that time, we told the British parliament that we were not ready to break this last colonial link.

'The constitution of Canada has come home'

After 50 years of discussion we have finally decided to retrieve what is properly ours . . . It is my deepest hope that Canada will match its own legal maturity with that degree of political maturity which will allow us all to make a total commitment to the Canadian ideal.

I speak of a Canada where men and women of aboriginal ancestry, of French and British heritage, of the diverse cultures of the world, demonstrate the will to share this land in peace, in justice and with mutual respect. I speak of a Canada which is proud of and strengthened by its essential bilingual destiny, a Canada whose people believe in sharing and in mutual support, and not in building regional barriers. I speak of a country where every person is free to fulfil himself or herself to the utmost, unhindered by the arbitrary actions of governments.

The Canadian ideal which we have tried to live, with varying degrees of success and failure for a hundred years, is really an act of defiance against the history of mankind. Had this country been founded upon a less noble vision, or had our forefathers surrendered to the difficulties of building this nation, Canada would have been torn apart long ago. It should not surprise us, therefore, that even now we sometimes feel the pull of those old reflexes of mutual fear and distrust: fear of becoming vulnerable by opening one's arms to other Canadians who speak a different language or live in a different culture; fear of becoming poorer by agreeing to share one's resources and wealth with fellow citizens living in a region less favoured by nature.

> ## 'Had our forefathers surrendered to the difficulties of building this nation, Canada would have been torn apart long ago'

The Canada we are building lies beyond the horizon of such fears. Yet it is not, for all that, an unreal country, forgetful of the hearts of men and women. We know that justice and generosity can flourish only in an atmosphere of trust.

For if individuals and minorities do not feel protected against the possibility of the tyranny of the majority, if French-speaking Canadians or Native peoples or new Canadians do not feel they will be treated with justice, it is useless to ask them to open their hearts and minds to their fellow Canadians. Similarly, if provinces feel that their sovereign rights are not secure in those fields in which they have full constitutional jurisdiction, it is useless to preach to them about cooperation and sharing.

The constitution which is being proclaimed today goes a long way toward removing the reasons for the fears of which I have spoken. We now have a charter which . . . guarantees the basic rights and freedoms which each of us shall enjoy as a citizen of Canada.

It reinforces the protection offered to French-speaking Canadians outside Quebec, and to English-speaking Canadians in Quebec. It recognizes our multicultural character. It upholds the equality of women, and the rights of disabled persons.

The constitution confirms the long-standing division of powers among governments in Canada, and even strengthens provincial jurisdiction over natural resources and property rights. It entrenches the principle of equalization, thus helping less wealthy provinces to discharge their obligations without excessive taxation. It offers a way to meet the legitimate demands of our Native peoples. And, of course, by its amending formula, it now permits us to complete the task of constitutional renewal in Canada.

The government of Quebec decided that it wasn't enough. It decided not to participate in this ceremony, celebrating Canada's full independence. I know that many Quebecers feel themselves pulled in two directions by that decision. But one need look only at the results of the referendum in May 1980 to realize how strong is the attachment to Canada among the people of Quebec. By definition, the silent majority does not make a lot of noise; it is content to make history.

History will show, however, that in the guarantees written into the Charter of Rights and Freedoms, and in the amending formula, which allows Quebec to opt out of any constitutional arrangement which touches upon language and culture, with full financial compensation, nothing essential to the originality of Quebec has been sacrificed . . .

'We now have a charter which . . . guarantees the basic rights and freedoms which each of us shall enjoy as a citizen of Canada'

It must, however, be recognized that no constitution, no charter of rights and freedoms, no sharing of powers can be a substitute for the willingness to share the risks and grandeur of the Canadian adventure. Without that collective act of the will, our constitution would be a dead letter, and our country would wither away.

It is true that our will to live together has sometimes appeared to be in deep hibernation; but it is there nevertheless, alive and tenacious, in the hearts of Canadians of every province and territory. I wish simply that the bringing home of our constitution marks the end of a long winter, the breaking-up of the ice jams and the beginning of a new spring.

For what we are celebrating today is not so much the completion of our task, but the renewal of our hope; not so much an ending, but a fresh beginning. Let us celebrate the renewal and repatriation of our constitution; but let us put our faith, first and foremost, in the people of Canada, who will breathe life into it.

'*I warn you that you will have pain*'

Neil Kinnock

(b. 1942)

THE RISING STAR OF THE LABOUR PARTY SPEAKS ON THE EVE OF THE
1983 GENERAL ELECTION; BRIDGEND, SOUTH WALES, 7 JUNE 1983

'I warn you that you will have pain'

S ocial conflict, ideological economics and strident rhetoric marked the end of Britain's postwar consensus during Margaret Thatcher's premiership and belied the country's reputation for moderation, centrism and civility. The Conservative government elected in 1979 inherited an economy weakened by persistent strikes and plagued by high levels of unemployment and inflation, and it had sought to cure these ailments by pursuing 'free-market' policies. Neil Kinnock's warning, delivered during the 1983 general election, was based on the ensuing aggravation of social misery, especially in those areas of Britain, such as his own southeast Wales, where heavy industry had already been in steady decline for over two decades. An application of 'monetarism' – the belief that the money supply was inflation's sole determinant – had proved especially witless and reflected the prime minister's susceptibility to dogma. Monetarist counsel indicated that high interest rates would moderate a growth in the money supply and so reduce inflation. Experience contra-dicted theory and inflation continued to rise until the Thatcher U-turn of late 1981, when monetarism was abandoned and interest rates were reduced. Inflation began to fall, but by then an immense cost had been inflicted.

Labour's legacy of a million unemployed first of all doubled in the early 1980s and would then peak at 3.6 million. By 1983 manufacturing output had suffered a massive 30 per cent reduction compared to its level of five years earlier. Britain's underlying problem of an uncompetitive economy had resisted politicians' aspiring solutions since at least 1945. Kinnock spoke for the many who considered the Tory cure to be worse than the original

NEIL KINNOCK (b. 1942)

1965 Graduates from University of Wales, Cardiff

1966–70 Tutor at Workers' Educational Association.

1970 Elected MP (Labour) for Bedwellty (subsequently Islwyn), South Wales.

1979 Leads successful campaign against Labour government's proposals for Welsh devolution.

May 1979 Labour government defeated; subsequently joins Shadow Cabinet as Education spokesman.

Oct 1983 Elected Labour leader following party's general election defeat.

1987 Conservative government elected with majority of 101.

July 1992 Resigns as Labour leader following Conservative election victory with majority of 21.

1995–2004 Member of European Union Commission despite hostility to European integration in the 1970s.

1999–2004 Vice president of EU Commission.

2004 Appointed Chairman of the British Council.

2005 Becomes Baron Kinnock of Bedwellty, despite hostility to existence of House of Lords in the 1970s.

disease but whose numbers failed to prevent the government's re-election in 1983 with a 144 majority – though only 42.4 per cent actually voted Conservative.

The Labour Party which subsequently elected Kinnock to lead it was at a spectacularly low ebb. Those in work were benefiting from the return of economic growth, and the Thatcher cult of leadership had been emboldened by her zest during the Falklands War of 1982, when British forces retook the South Atlantic islands following an Argentinian invasion. Members of the far-left Militant Tendency had infiltrated Labour ranks and associated the party with extremism, while the formation of the Social Democratic Party had divided the British centre-left vote and thereby boosted the Tory majority. The personal edge to political debate was aggravated by pro-Thatcher newspaper editors who encouraged attacks on Kinnock's animated personality and verbose tendencies. Throughout these travails he remained resilient and often witty, and despite his left-wing origins Kinnock understood how and why his party had to change. Addressing the Labour conference in 1985, he attacked the local authority in Liverpool where Militant's influence had resulted in 'the grotesque chaos of a Labour council . . . hiring taxis to scuttle round a city handing out redundancy notices to its own workers'. By the 1987 election Labour had purged itself of such extremism and attained some aplomb in its communication and self-presentation, though its defeat of that year, like that of 1992, showed that preaching the need for 'the collective effort of the whole community' was a hard task in a post-socialist age.

'

If Margaret Thatcher is re-elected as prime minister, I warn you

I warn you that you will have pain –

When healing and relief depend upon payment.

I warn you that you will have ignorance –

When talents are untended and wits are wasted, when learning is a privilege and not a right.

I warn you that you will have poverty –

When pensions slip and benefits are whittled away by a government that won't pay in an economy that can't pay.

I warn you that you will be cold –

When fuel charges are used as a tax system that the rich don't notice and the poor can't afford.

I warn you that you must not expect work –

When many cannot spend, more will not be able to earn. When they don't earn, they don't spend. When they don't spend, work dies.

I warn you not to go into the streets alone after dark or into the streets in large crowds of protest in the light.

'I warn you not to go into the streets alone after dark or into the streets in large crowds of protest in the light'

I warn you that you will be quiet –

When the curfew of fear and the gibbet of unemployment make you obedient.

I warn you that you will have defence of a sort –

With a risk and at a price that passes all understanding.

I warn you that you will be home-bound –

When fares and transport bills kill leisure and lock you up.

I warn you that you will borrow less –

When credit, loans, mortgages and easy payments are refused to people on your melting income.

'If Margaret Thatcher wins I warn you not to be ordinary'

If Margaret Thatcher wins, she will be more a leader than a prime minister. That power produces arrogance, and when it is toughened by Tebbitry and flattered and fawned upon by spineless sycophants, the boot-licking tabloid Knights of Fleet Street and placemen . . . the arrogance corrupts absolutely.

If Margaret Thatcher wins –

I warn you not to be ordinary.

I warn you not to be young.

I warn you not to fall ill.

I warn you not to get old.

'We are democratic socialists. We care all the time'

THE LABOUR LEADER ADDRESSES THE PARTY FAITHFUL IN THE RUN-UP TO THE 1987 GENERAL ELECTION; LLANDUDNO, NORTH WALES, 15 MAY 1987

We are democratic socialists. We care all the time. We don't think it's a soft sentiment, we don't think it's 'wet'.

We think that care is the essence of strength.

And we believe that because we know that strength without care is savage and brutal and selfish.

Strength with care is compassion – the practical action that is needed to help people lift themselves to their full stature . . .

But where do we get that strength to provide that care?

Do we wait for some stroke of good fortune, some benign giant, some socially conscious Samson to come along and pick up the wretched of the earth?

Of course we don't.

We cooperate, we collect together, we coordinate so that everyone can contribute and everyone can benefit, everyone has responsibilities, everyone has rights . . . That is how we make the weak strong, that is how we lift the needy, that is how we make the sick whole, that is how we give talent the chance to flourish, that is how we turn the unemployed claimant into the working contributor . . .

When we speak of collective strength and collective freedom, collectively achieved, we are not fulfilling that nightmare that Mrs Thatcher tries to paint . . .

We're not talking about uniformity; we're not talking about regimentation; we're not talking about conformity – that's their creed. The uniformity of the dole queue; the regimentation of the unemployed young and their compulsory work schemes. The conformity of people who will work in conditions, and take orders, and accept pay because of mass unemployment that they would laugh at in a free society with full employment.

That kind of freedom for the individual . . . can't be secured by most of the people for most of the time if they're just left to themselves, isolated, stranded, with their whole life chances dependent upon luck! . . .

NEIL KINNOCK   139

'We are democratic socialists. We care all the time'

And now, Mrs Thatcher, by dint of privatization, and means test, and deprivation, and division, wants to nudge us back into the situation where everybody can either stand on their own feet, or live on their knees.

That's what this election is about as she parades her visions and values, and we choose to contest them as people with roots in this country, with a future only in this country, with pride in this country. People who know that if we are to have and sustain real individual liberty in this country, it requires the collective effort of the whole community.

Of course you hear the Tories talking about freedom. We'll be hearing a great deal of that over the next month from the same people who have spent the last eight years crushing individual freedoms under the weight of unemployment and poverty, squeezing individual rights with cuts and means tests and charges.

'They live in a free country, but they do not feel free'

I think of the youngsters I meet. Three, four, five years out of school. Never had a job. And they say to me, 'Do you think we'll ever work?'

They live in a free country, but they do not feel free.

I think of the 55-year-old woman I meet who is waiting to go into hospital, her whole existence clouded by pain . . .

And I think of the old couple who spend months of the winter afraid to turn up the heating, who stay at home because they are afraid to go out after dark, whose lives are turned into a crisis by the need to buy a new pair of shoes.

They live in a free country . . . but they do not feel free.

How can they – and millions like them – have their individual freedom if there is no collective provision?

How can they have strength if they do not have care?

Now they cannot have either because they are locked out of being able to discharge responsibilities just as surely as they are locked out of being able to exercise rights.

They want to be able to use both.

They do not want feather-bedding, they want a foothold.

They do not want cotton-woolling, they want a chance to contribute.

That is the freedom they want.

That is the freedom we want them to have.

'Isolationism never was and never will be an acceptable response to tyrannical governments'

Ronald Reagan

(1911–2004)

THE AMERICAN PRESIDENT MARKS THE 40TH ANNIVERSARY OF THE D-DAY LANDINGS; US RANGER MONUMENT, POINTE DU HOC, FRANCE, 6 JUNE 1984

'Isolationism never was and never will be an acceptable response to tyrannical governments'

I n the summer of 1984 Ronald Reagan was running for re-election, and this superbly crafted speech, written by the president's special assistant Peggy Noonan, encapsulated his administration's consistent foreign-policy goals. The commemoration of the D-Day landings required a particular tone of moral gravity blending sorrow with pride, remembrance of lives lost in battle as well as confidence in the justice of the Allied cause. Noonan's words and Reagan's faultless delivery avoided mere triumphalism and made a necessary connection: totalitarianism's fascist form had been defeated in 1944–5 but its communist expression continued to divide Europe. Freedom's business remained unfinished.

Reagan's own military service was of a specialized kind. In 1937, the year he signed a seven-year contract with Warner Brothers, Reagan enlisted in the US Army Reserve and was commissioned as a second lieutenant. Near-sightedness disqualified him from overseas service, and in 1942 he was assigned to the public relations division of the Army Air Force, working subsequently for the California-based First Motion Picture Unit. Reagan's critics mocked him as a mere B-movie actor whose second profession of politics provided him with an alternative theatre for the delivery of other people's words. This missed the point. Reagan's belief that communism was unnatural as well as wicked was genuine and not contrived, and his words were taken seriously because he clearly believed in them and acted accordingly. The USSR was an 'evil empire' (June 1982) tottering towards extinction and communism in general was 'another sad, bizarre chapter in human history whose last pages even now are being written' (March 1983). The sunny and optimistic temperament of this natural Californian helped him gain support for these militant assertions, and mockery as well as excoriation were well within his dramatic range.

RONALD REAGAN (1911–2004)

1947–52, 1959 President of the Screen Actors Guild.

1962 Switches allegiance from the Democratic Party to the Republicans.

1966 Elected governor of California and serves in office, 1967–75.

1976 Campaigns for the Republican presidential nomination but is defeated by the incumbent Gerald Ford.

1980 Gains Republican nomination and is elected US president.

1984 Re-elected president.

1986 Details emerge of covert arms sales to Iran to fund anti-communist Contra insurgents in Nicaragua, a policy specifically outlawed by Congress; 14 of his staff are subsequently indicted and 11 convicted.

Jan 1989 Leaves office.

1993 Awarded Presidential Medal of Freedom.

Nov 1994 Makes public that he is suffering from Alzheimer's disease.

Past, present and future are intercut to dramatic, even filmic, effect as the speech proceeds from its evocation of the beachhead scene of 40 years ago to the concluding peroration linking historic sacrifice with contemporary struggle and battles yet to be won. There is poetry, too, when the scene shifts across the Atlantic to the pen portrait of a prayerful hush as news of the invasion spreads through an expectant America. The speech is grounded in recollected emotion and renewed gratitude for valour displayed in a noble cause, and the connection made with its immediate audience of veterans is both poignant and dignified.

Soviet communism's collapse showed that America's hostile words worked – but money also talked. Reagan's first term saw a 40 per cent real-terms increase in the defence budget, and in 1983 he unveiled the Strategic Defence Initiative (SDI), a ground- and space-based system intended to provide the US with a defence shield against nuclear ballistic missiles. Though never fully developed, SDI's prevision of a US rendered invulnerable to nuclear attack alarmed the USSR, since it abolished any notion of an equivalence of offensive capacity. The fall of the Berlin Wall in 1989 signified the collapse of Soviet communism and of its satellite governments in Central and Eastern Europe. Regan's prediction had come true, and the US was the only superpower left.

'We're here to mark that day in history when the Allied armies joined in battle to reclaim this continent for liberty . . . Here the Allies stood and fought against tyranny in a giant undertaking unparalleled in human history.

We stand on a lonely, windswept point on the northern shore of France. The air is soft, but 40 years ago at this moment, the air was dense with smoke and the cries of men, and the air was filled with the crack of rifle fire and the roar of cannon. At dawn, on the morning of 6 June 1944, 225 Rangers jumped off the British landing craft and ran to the bottom of these cliffs. Their mission was one of the most difficult and daring of the invasion: to climb these sheer and desolate cliffs and take out the enemy guns.

The Rangers looked up and saw the enemy soldiers shooting down at them with machine guns and throwing grenades. And the American Rangers began to climb . . . Soon, one by one, the Rangers pulled themselves over the top, and in seizing the firm land at the top of these cliffs, they began to seize back the continent of Europe. Two hundred and twenty-five came here. After two days of fighting, only 90 could still bear arms.

Behind me is a memorial that symbolizes the Ranger daggers that were thrust into the top of these cliffs. And before me are the men who put them there . . .

'What inspired all the men of the armies that met here?'

Forty summers have passed since the battle that you fought here. You were young the day
you took these cliffs; some of you were hardly more than boys, with the deepest joys of life
before you. Yet, you risked everything here . . . What inspired all the men of the armies that
met here? We look at you, and somehow we know the answer. It was faith and belief; it was
loyalty and love.

'There is a profound, moral difference between the use of force for liberation and the use of force for conquest'

The men of Normandy had faith that what they were doing was right, faith that they fought
for all humanity, faith that a just God would grant them mercy on this beachhead or on the
next. It was the deep knowledge – and pray God we have not lost it – that there is a
profound, moral difference between the use of force for liberation and the use of force for
conquest. You were here to liberate, not to conquer, and so you and those others did not
doubt your cause. And you were right not to doubt.

You all knew that some things are worth dying for. One's country is worth dying for, and
democracy is worth dying for, because it's the most deeply honourable form of government
ever devised by man. All of you loved liberty. All of you were willing to fight tyranny, and
you knew the people of your countries were behind you.

The Americans who fought here that morning knew word of the invasion was spreading
through the darkness back home. They felt in their hearts . . . that in Georgia they were
filling the churches at 4 a.m., in Kansas they were kneeling on their porches and praying,
and in Philadelphia they were ringing the Liberty Bell . . .

'The Allies summoned strength from the faith, belief, loyalty and love of those who fell here'

When the war was over, there were lives to be rebuilt and governments to be returned to the
people. There were nations to be reborn. Above all, there was a new peace to be assured.
These were huge and daunting tasks. But the Allies summoned strength from the faith,
belief, loyalty and love of those who fell here. They rebuilt a new Europe together . . .

In spite of our great efforts and successes, not all that followed the end of the war was happy
or planned. Some liberated countries were lost. The great sadness of this loss echoes down to
our own time in the streets of Warsaw, Prague and East Berlin. Soviet troops that came to the

centre of this continent did not leave when peace came. They're still there, uninvited, unwanted, unyielding, almost 40 years after the war. Because of this, Allied forces still stand on this continent. Today, as 40 years ago, our armies are here for only one purpose – to protect and defend democracy . . .

We in America have learned bitter lessons from two world wars: it is better to be here ready to protect the peace than to take blind shelter across the sea, rushing to respond only after freedom is lost. We've learned that isolationism never was and never will be an acceptable response to tyrannical governments with an expansionist intent.

But we try always to be prepared for peace; prepared to deter aggression; prepared to negotiate the reduction of arms; and, yes, prepared to reach out again in the spirit of reconciliation . . .

It's fitting to remember here the great losses also suffered by the Russian people during World War II: 20 million perished, a terrible price . . . I tell you from my heart that we in the United States do not want war. We want to wipe from the face of the earth the terrible weapons that man now has in his hands. And I tell you, we are ready to seize that beachhead. We look for some sign from the Soviet Union that they are willing to move forward, that they share our desire and love for peace, and that they will give up the ways of conquest . . .

We will pray forever that some day that changing will come. But for now, particularly today, it is good and fitting to renew our commitment to each other, to our freedom, and to the alliance that protects it.

> ## 'We want to wipe from the face of the earth the terrible weapons that man now has in his hands'

We are bound today by what bound us 40 years ago, the same loyalties, traditions and beliefs. We're bound by reality. The strength of America's allies is vital to the United States, and the American security guarantee is essential to the continued freedom of Europe's democracies.

Here, in this place where the West held together, let us make a vow to our dead. Let us show them by our actions that we understand what they died for . . .

Strengthened by their courage . . . let us continue to stand for the ideals for which they lived and died.

'For the love of God: Please, make this nation remember how futures are built'

Mario Cuomo

(b. 1932)

THE GOVERNOR OF NEW YORK CALLS THE DEMOCRATS BACK TO THEIR CORE VALUES; DEMOCRATIC PARTY NATIONAL CONVENTION, SAN FRANCISCO, 16 JULY 1984

The 1980s were not the Democrats' decade. Jimmy Carter's evident decency and earnestness helped them regain the presidency in 1976, but the latter part of his period in office was overshadowed by the Iran hostage crisis. Islamic fundamentalists had stormed the US embassy in Tehran, where for 444 days they detained 52 American diplomats and were initially impervious to negotiation. Carter's inability to secure their release seemed to denote a more general loss of US authority in world affairs and the Democrats paid an electoral price. Hostility to federal expenditure, lower taxation and an aggressively anti-communist foreign policy: these were the keynotes of 1980s politics as provided by a resurgent Republican Party. The fact that the Iranians delayed the hostages' release until the first day of the Reagan presidency compounded the Democratic humiliation.

Democrats needed, therefore, some additional inspiration at their 1984 convention, and it was Mario Cuomo's address that provided them with a cogent reminder of their core values. He was already a popular figure with those liberal Democrats who admired his blend of compassion and efficiency. He consistently delivered a balanced budget during his 12 years as New York's governor and there were even occasional tax cuts. Public-sector investment spurred the private sector's economic development and job creation. Cuomo's gubernatorial budget expanded housing programmes for the homeless, funded treatment centres for drug addicts, and was notably pioneering in its provision for those suffering from AIDS and mental illness. This made his state into a surviving beacon of liberal values in an American political landscape being reshaped by a vigorous Republicanism. It was John Winthrop, the governor of the Massachusetts Bay Company, who coined the phrase 'city upon a hill' in a sermon of 1630, and Reagan's version of the phrase expressed a similar sense of America's exemplary destiny. Cuomo's extension of the metaphor portrayed the divisive consequences of 'Reaganomics' to graphic effect and led many to hope that he would run for the presidency.

MARIO CUOMO (b. 1932)

1953 Graduates from St John's University, New York City, a Catholic university from which he also graduates (1956) in law.

1956 Called to the New York bar.

1958 Enters legal practice.

1975 Appointed New York's Secretary of State by Governor Hugh Carey.

1978 Elected lieutenant governor of New York.

1982 Elected governor of New York, and serves three consecutive terms after being re-elected in 1986 and 1990.

1987 Announces that he will not contest the Democratic Party's nomination for the US presidency.

1994 Stands for re-election as governor defeated by Republican George Pataki.

When Carter left office, inflation was running at almost 12 per cent and unemployment stood at 7.5 per cent. The Republican corrective included large tax cuts which stimulated economic growth but limited government revenue. By 1984 Reagan was running an annual federal budget deficit of 200 billion dollars, and his eventual legacy included a national debt which increased from 700 billion to 3 trillion dollars. The background to Cuomo's speech, therefore, was the major recession of 1982 in the course of which American unemployment peaked at 10.8 per cent, although two years later it was evident that the economy was once again expanding. A total of 16 million new jobs were created during Reagan's presidency and US GDP grew at an annual rate of just over 3 per cent. But the recession had had an especially grievous impact on the urban poor, who found an eloquent advocate and defender in New York's governor. Cuomo's parents were Italian immigrants and his father had worked as a cleaner of sewers while saving enough money to open a grocery store in the New York borough of Queens. These struggles, and his family's Catholicism, made a profound impression on this unusually introspective politician, whose call to conscience expresses his intense conviction that 'the family of America' is built on inclusion and endeavour.

Ten days ago, President Reagan admitted that although some people in this country seemed to be doing well nowadays, others were unhappy, even worried . . . The president said that he didn't understand that fear. He said: 'Why, this country is a shining city on a hill.' And the president is right. In many ways we are a shining city on a hill.

But . . . there's another part to the shining city; the part where people can't pay their mortgages . . . ; where students can't afford the education they need and middle-class parents watch the dreams they hold for their children evaporate.

In this part of the city there are more poor than ever . . . And there are people who sleep in the city streets, in the gutter, where the glitter doesn't show . . . There is despair, Mr President, in the faces that you don't see, in the places that you don't visit . . .

'There are people who sleep in the city streets, in the gutter, where the glitter doesn't show'

The truth is that this is how we were warned it would be . . . 'Government can't do everything,' we were told, so it should settle for taking care of the strong and hope that economic ambition and charity will do the rest . . .

The difference between Democrats and Republicans has always been measured in courage and confidence. The Republicans believe that the wagon train will not make it to the frontier unless some of the old, some of the young, some of the weak are left behind by the side of the trail . . . We Democrats believe that we can make it all the way with the whole family intact . . .

Today our great Democratic Party, which has saved the nation from depression, from fascism, from racism, from corruption, is called upon to do it again – this time to save the nation from confusion and division, from the threat of eventual fiscal disaster, and most of all from the fear of a nuclear holocaust . . .

What chance would the Republican candidate have had in 1980 if he had told the American people that he intended to pay for his so-called economic recovery with bankruptcies, unemployment, more homeless, more hungry, and the largest government debt known to humankind? . . .

They said that they would make us and the whole world safer. They say they have: by creating the largest defence budget in history; by escalating to a frenzy the nuclear arms race; by incendiary rhetoric; by refusing to discuss peace with our enemies . . .

'We give money to Latin American governments that murder nuns, and then we lie about it'

We give money to Latin American governments that murder nuns, and then we lie about it . . . Our foreign policy drifts with no real direction, other than an hysterical commitment to an arms race that leads nowhere – if we're lucky. And if we're not, it could lead us into bankruptcy or war . . .

Where would another four years take us? . . .

We must ask ourselves what kind of country will be fashioned by the man who believes . . . that the laws against discrimination against people go too far; a man who threatens Social Security and Medicaid and help for the disabled. How high will we pile the missiles? . . .

We Democrats believe in a government strong enough to use words like 'love' and 'compassion' and smart enough to convert our noblest aspirations into practical realities . . .

We believe that while survival of the fittest may be a good working description of the process of evolution, a government of humans should elevate itself to a higher order.

'We Democrats believe in a government strong enough to use words like "love" and "compassion"'

Our government should be able to rise to the level where it can fill the gaps that are left by chance or by a wisdom we don't fully understand. We would rather have laws written by the patron of this great city, St Francis of Assisi, than laws written by Darwin . . .

We believe in a single fundamental idea that describes . . . what a proper government should be: the idea of family, mutuality, the sharing of benefits and burdens for the good of all . . . without respect to race, or sex, or geography, or political affiliation.

We believe that we must be the family of America, recognizing that at the heart of the matter we are bound one to another . . .

We Democrats created a better future for our children, using traditional Democratic principles as a fixed beacon, giving us direction and purpose, but constantly innovating, adapting to new realities . . .

We can do it again, if we do not forget that this entire nation has profited by these progressive principles; that they helped lift up generations to the middle class and higher; that they gave us a chance to work, to go to college, to raise a family, to own a house, to be secure in our old age . . .

'We Democrats created a better future for our children, using traditional Democratic principles as a fixed beacon'

The struggle to live with dignity is the real story of the shining city. And it's a story that I didn't read in a book, or learn in a classroom. I saw it and lived it, like many of you. I watched a small man with thick calluses on both his hands work 15 and 16 hours a day. I saw him once literally bleed from the bottoms of his feet, a man who came here uneducated, alone, unable to speak the language, who taught me all I needed to know about faith and hard work by the simple eloquence of his example. I learned about our kind of democracy from my father. And I learned about our obligation to each other from him and from my mother. They asked for a chance to work and to make the world better for their children, and they asked to be protected in those moments when they would not be able to protect themselves. This nation and this nation's government did that for them.

And that they were able to build a family and live in dignity and see one of their children . . . occupy the highest seat, in the greatest state, in the greatest nation, in the only world we would know, is an ineffably beautiful tribute to the democratic process.

And on 20 January 1985 it will happen again – only on a much, much grander scale. We will have a new president of the United States, a Democrat . . .

It will happen if we make it happen; if you and I make it happen. And I ask you now, for the good of all of us, for the love of this great nation, for the family of America, for the love of God: Please, make this nation remember how futures are built.

'*Suffering breeds character. Character breeds faith. In the end, faith will not disappoint*'

Jesse Jackson
(b. 1941)

THE DEFEATED CANDIDATE FOR THE DEMOCRATIC NOMINATION FOR THE
US PRESIDENCY ADDRESSES HIS PARTY'S NATIONAL CONVENTION;
SAN FRANCISCO, 18 JULY 1984

'Suffering breeds character. Character breeds faith.
In the end, faith will not disappoint'

J esse Jackson emerged as the civil rights movement's most significant leader during the years following the assassination of his mentor Martin Luther King, Jr. He too had been ordained into the Baptist ministry, and although his lush oratory lacked King's intellectual focus, Jackson communicated a direct passion which made a powerful impact on the Democratic Party. He was not the first African-American to contest the presidency, but Congresswoman Shirley Chisholm's 1972 campaign for the Democratic nomination had been largely symbolic. Jackson had no experience at this stage of elective public office and most observers thought initially that his presidential ambitions lacked a serious intent. Moreover, his aim of reversing tax cuts, reducing defence expenditure and expanding welfare went against the emergent political consensus. But a campaign conducted with typical verve gained Jackson 18.2 per cent of the total votes cast during the Democratic primaries, and the result ensured his subsequent status as a major force within his party. His feel for the Democrats' recent history undoubtedly helped him in this regard and is illustrated by this speech's reference to Hubert Humphrey. The former vice president (1965–9), defeated by Richard Nixon in the presidential election of 1968, was admired for his progressivism and fortitude, and the widespread feeling that Humphrey was the Democrats' great lost leader had survived his support for the war in Vietnam.

The need for black Americans to work together as part of a wider coalition was a major aspect of the King legacy. This included the furthering of North–South solidarity among civil rights activists, and in 1966 King asked Jackson to assume responsibility for the expansion into Chicago of the protests organized by the Southern Christian Leadership Conference (SCLC). Ralph Abernathy, who became head of the SCLC after King's assassination, clashed repeatedly with Jackson, who therefore decided to resign from the organization in December 1971 and to form his own movement. The result was Operation PUSH (People United to Save Humanity), a Chicago-based body which concentrated on

JESSE JACKSON (b. 1941)

1966 Leaves Chicago Theological Seminary to become a full-time civil rights activist.

1968 Ordained a Baptist minister.

Nov 1983 Announces candidacy for Democratic presidential nomination.

1984 Walter Mondale, Democratic presidential nominee, is defeated and President Reagan re-elected.

1988 Gains 6.9 million votes in the Democratic primaries as candidate for the

presidential nomination; Vice President George Bush, the Republican candidate, defeats the Democrats' nominee Michael Dukakis.

1991–7 Shadow senator for the District of Columbia, an elective office whose holder lobbies for the District's admission as a Union state.

2000 Awarded Medal of Freedom by President Clinton.

promoting African-Americans' business opportunities and employment rights. In 1984 Jackson founded another movement, the Rainbow Coalition, which represented a very wide spectrum of interest groups. His description in this speech of an American quilt formed out of diversity but united by a common thread indicates the range of the Coalition, and in 1996, under his continued leadership, Jackson's two organizations merged.

Occasional diplomatic forays confirmed Jackson's patriotism. In 1983 he secured the release of an American pilot captured by the Syrians, and in the month before this speech's delivery he had negotiated the release of 22 US citizens being detained in Cuba. The acclaim that greeted his 1984 address and Jackson's subsequent energy in renewing, regrouping and moving on provided him with a springboard for another attempt at gaining the Democratic presidential nomination in 1988, when he gained 21 per cent of the vote in the party's primaries. But the emergence of Michael Dukakis, governor of Massachusetts, as the lacklustre party nominee showed the limits to the powers of persuasion that could be exerted even by Jackson's dazzling verbal pyrotechnics.

‘This is not a perfect party. We are not a perfect people. Yet, we are called to a perfect mission. Our mission: to feed the hungry; to clothe the naked; to house the homeless; to teach the illiterate; to provide jobs for the jobless; and to choose the human race over the nuclear race.

We are gathered here this week to nominate a candidate and adopt a platform which will expand, unify, direct and inspire our party and the nation to fulfil this mission. My constituency is the desperate, the damned, the disinherited, the disrespected and the despised. They are restless and seek relief . . .

Leadership must heed the call of conscience, redemption, expansion, healing and unity . . . Throughout this campaign, I've tried to offer leadership to the Democratic Party and the nation. If, in my high moments, I have done some good, offered some service, shed some light, healed some wounds, rekindled some hope, or stirred someone from apathy and indifference . . . then this campaign has not been in vain.

If, in my low moments, . . . I have caused anyone discomfort, created pain or revived someone's fears, that was not my truest self . . . Please forgive me. I am not a perfect servant. I am a public servant doing my best against the odds. As I develop and serve, be patient: God is not finished with me yet . . .

I went to see Hubert Humphrey three days before he died. He had just called Richard Nixon from his dying bed, and many people wondered why. And I asked him. He said: 'Jesse, from this vantage point, the sun is setting in my life, all of the speeches, the political conventions, the crowds and the great fights are behind me now. At a time like this you are forced to deal with your irreducible essence, forced to grapple with that which is really important to you. And what I've concluded about life,' Hubert Humphrey said, 'When all is said and done, we must forgive each other, and redeem each other, and move on.'

'Suffering breeds character. Character breeds faith.
In the end, faith will not disappoint'

Our party is emerging from one of its most hard-fought battles for the Democratic Party's presidential nomination in our history. But our healthy competition should make us better, not bitter. We must use the insight, wisdom and experience of the late Hubert Humphrey as a balm for the wounds in our party, this nation and the world. We must forgive each other, redeem each other, regroup and move on.

'We must forgive each other, redeem each other, regroup and move on'

America is not like a blanket – one piece of unbroken cloth, the same colour, the same texture, the same size. America is more like a quilt: many patches, many pieces, many colours, many sizes, all woven and held together by a common thread. The white, the Hispanic, the black, the Arab, the Jew, the woman, the native American, the small farmer, the businessperson, the environmentalist, the peace activist, the young, the old, the lesbian, the gay and the disabled make up the American quilt.

Even in our fractured state, all of us count and fit somewhere. We have proven that we can survive without each other. But we have not proven that we can win and make progress without each other. We must come together . . .

The requirement for rebuilding America is justice. The linchpin of progressive politics in our nation will not come from the North; they, in fact, will come from the South . . .

If blacks vote in great numbers, progressive whites win. It's the only way progressive whites win. If blacks vote in great numbers, Hispanics win. When blacks, Hispanics and progressive whites vote, women win. When women win, children win. When women and children win, workers win. We must all come up together . . .

'There is a way out – jobs. Put America back to work'

There is a way out – jobs. Put America back to work. When I was a child growing up in Greenville, South Carolina, the Reverend Sample used to preach every so often a sermon relating to Jesus. And he said: 'If I be lifted up, I'll draw all men unto me.' I didn't quite understand what he meant as a child growing up, but I understand a little better now. If you raise up truth, it's magnetic. It has a way of drawing people . . .

If we lift up a programme to feed the hungry, they'll come running; if we lift up a programme to study war no more, our youth will come running; if we lift up a programme to put America back to work, and an alternative to welfare and despair, they will come running . . .

'You must face reality – that which is. But then dream of a reality that ought to be – that must be'

In this campaign, I've tried to be faithful to my promise. I lived in old barrios, ghettos, and reservations and housing projects. I have a message for our youth. I challenge them to put hope in their brains and not dope in their veins . . . Just because you're born in the slum does not mean the slum is born in you, and you can rise above it if your mind is made up . . .

I'm more convinced than ever that we can win. We will vault up the rough side of the mountain. We can win. I just want young America to do me one favour, just one favour. Exercise the right to dream. You must face reality – that which is. But then dream of a reality that ought to be – that must be . . . Use hope and imagination as weapons of survival and progress. Use love to motivate you and obligate you to serve the human family.

'We must leave racial battle ground and come to economic common ground and moral higher ground'

Our time has come. Our time has come. Suffering breeds character. Character breeds faith. In the end, faith will not disappoint. Our time has come. Our faith, hope and dreams will prevail. Our time has come. Weeping has endured for nights, but now joy cometh in the morning. Our time has come. No grave can hold our body down. Our time has come. No lie can live forever. Our time has come. We must leave racial battle ground and come to economic common ground and moral higher ground. America, our time has come. We come from disgrace to amazing grace. Our time has come. Give me your tired, give me your poor, your huddled masses who yearn to breathe free and come November, there will be change because our time has come.

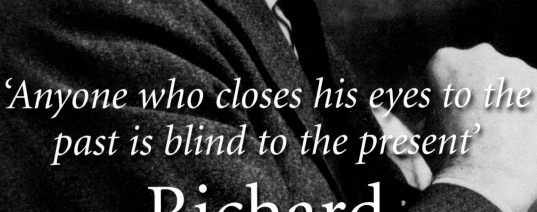

'*Anyone who closes his eyes to the past is blind to the present*'

Richard von Weizsäcker

(b. 1920)

THE PRESIDENT OF WEST GERMANY ADDRESSES THE BUNDESTAG ON THE 40TH
ANNIVERSARY OF THE END OF WAR IN EUROPE: BONN, 8 MAY 1985

This profound and measured account of guilt, innocence and suffering stands in the highest traditions of German, and European, statesmanship. President Richard von Weizsäcker was at this time West Germany's head of state, and that non-partisan role qualified him to speak on behalf of his compatriots. Personal experience lent an added significance to these words of a representative German.

The von Weizsäckers had given distinguished service to the Second Reich created in 1871, and the president's grandfather, state premier of Württemberg, was raised to the hereditary nobility in 1916. His father Ernst joined the German foreign office in 1920 and was ambassador to the Holy See from 1943 to 1945. In 1947 Ernst von Weizsäcker was arrested, charged with war crimes and, controversially, sentenced to a seven-year term of imprisonment by the US military tribunal held in Nuremberg. Richard von Weizsäcker, then a law student at Göttingen, acted as assistant defence counsel on behalf of his father, who was released as part of a general amnesty in 1950 but died the following year.

West Germany's rapid postwar development as a prosperous and stable democracy necessarily meant turning its back on the past. The 40th anniversary of the Third Reich's collapse was a public opportunity to start asking the question why Germany, at both an elite and a popular level, embraced totalitarianism in the interwar years. Some considered this process to be overdue, and student radicals in the 1960s had protested at the German establishment's indifference to the issues raised by the recent past. Von Weizsäcker's speech marked the start of a national self-examination which has continued ever since.

For the first time a senior German public figure stated explicitly that 8 May 1945 had been a 'day of liberation' for his compatriots. Given the scale of the national catastrophe, its anniversary could not be a day of celebration but it could be commemorated as 'the end of

RICHARD VON WEIZSÄCKER (b. 1920)

1939–45 Serves in the German army, and is wounded (1945) whilst campaigning in East Prussia.

1955 Gains his Juris Doctor, a professional doctorate in law, from University of Göttingen.

1967–84 Member of the Synod and Council of the German Evangelical (Lutheran) Church.

1954 Joins the Christian Democratic Union, a centre-right political party.

1969–81 Member of the Bundestag and (1979–81) its vice president.

1981–4 Governing mayor of West Berlin.

1984 Elected president of West Germany by the country's Federal Convention.

1989–94 Serves second term as president; presides over reunification of Germany and collapse of communist East Germany.

an aberration'. Germany's responsibility for starting the war is accepted, but the account of how the nation became the last victim of Nazism is both scrupulous and just: 'we became the victims of our own war.'

The personally cultivated and intellectually serious tone of this speech demonstrated qualities which had typified German society before Nazism and which re-emerged as distinguishing characteristics after 1945. Its religious emphasis is derived from von Weizsäcker's Protestant and Christian faith, an emphasis which explains why he thinks that 'Guilt is, like innocence, not collective, but personal.'

Western European moves towards a single currency and integrated political structures were gathering pace in the mid-1980s. Hence von Weizsäcker's subtle formulation: 'The new beginning . . . has brought both victory and defeat for the notion of freedom and self-determination.' The war was won by states who were defending their national independence. But avoiding its recurrence had involved a pooling of sovereignty. One reconciliation, however, that between East and West Germany, was yet to be achieved in 1985. Germany's return as 'one people and one nation', here prophesied, would become fact in just four years' time.

Many nations are today commemorating the date on which World War II ended in Europe. Be it victory or defeat, liberation from injustice and alien rule, or transition to new dependence, division, new alliances, vast shifts of power – 8 May 1945 is a date of decisive importance for Europe.

We Germans are commemorating that date among ourselves, as is indeed necessary. We must find our own standards. We are not assisted in this task if we or others spare our feelings.

For us Germans, 8 May is not a day of celebration. Those who actually witnessed that day in 1945 think back on highly personal and hence highly different experiences. Some returned home, others lost their homes. Some were liberated, while for others it was the start of captivity. Many were simply grateful that the bombing at night and fear had passed and that they had survived. Others felt first and foremost grief at the complete defeat suffered by their country. Some Germans felt bitterness about their shattered illusions, while others were grateful for the gift of a new start.

Most Germans had believed that they were fighting and suffering for the good of their country. And now it turned out that their efforts were not only in vain and futile, but had served the inhuman goals of a criminal regime.

'There is every reason for us to perceive 8 May 1945 as the end of an aberration in German history'

Yet with every day something became clearer, and this must be stated on behalf of all of us today. The eighth of May was a day of liberation. It liberated all of us from the inhumanity and tyranny of the National Socialist regime.

There is truly no reason for us today to participate in victory celebrations. But there is every reason for us to perceive 8 May 1945 as the end of an aberration in German history, an end bearing seeds of hope for a better future.

'There is no such thing as the guilt or innocence of an entire nation'

At the root of the tyranny was Hitler's immeasurable hatred against our Jewish compatriots. Hitler had never concealed this hatred from the public, but made the entire nation a tool of it . . . The genocide of the Jews is unparalleled in history. The nature and scope of the destruction may have exceeded human imagination, but in reality there was, apart from the crime itself, the attempt by too many people . . . not to take note of what was happening. There were too many ways of not burdening one's conscience, of shunning responsibility, looking away, keeping mum.

There is no such thing as the guilt or innocence of an entire nation. Guilt is, like innocence, not collective, but personal. Everyone who directly experienced that era should today quietly ask himself about his involvement then.

The vast majority of today's population were either children then or had not been born. No discerning person can expect them to wear a penitential robe simply because they are Germans. But their forefathers have left them a grave legacy.

'Remembrance is experience of the work of God in history'

It is not a case of coming to terms with the past. That is not possible. It cannot be subsequently modified or made not to have happened. However, anyone who closes his eyes to the past is blind to the present. Whoever refuses to remember the inhumanity is prone to new risks of infection.

'Seeking to forget makes exile all the longer. The secret of redemption lies in remembrance.' This Jewish adage surely expresses the idea that faith in God is faith in the work of God in history. Remembrance is experience of the work of God in history. It is the source of faith in redemption. This experience creates hope, creates faith in redemption, in reunification of the divided, in reconciliation.

Hitler wanted to dominate Europe and to do so through war. The Soviet Union was prepared for other nations to fight one another so that it could have a share of the spoils. The initiative for the war, however, came from Germany.

In the course of that war the Nazi regime tormented and defiled many nations. At the end of it all, only one nation remained to be tormented, enslaved and defiled: the German nation. Time and again Hitler had declared that if the German nation was not capable of winning the war, it should be left to perish. The other nations first became victims of a war started by Germany before we became the victims of our own war.

The new beginning in Europe after 1945 has brought both victory and defeat for the notion of freedom and self-determination. Our aim is to seize the opportunity to draw a line under a long period of European history in which to every country peace seemed conceivable and safe only as a result of its own supremacy, and in which peace meant a period of preparation for the next war.

> ## 'Other nations first became victims of a war started by Germany before we became the victims of our own war'

Whereas at the end of the war many Germans tried to hide their passports or to exchange them for another one, German nationality today is highly valued. We may look back with gratitude on our development over these 40 years, if we use the memory of our own history as a guideline for our future behaviour.

– If we remember that mentally disturbed persons were put to death in the Third Reich, we will see care of people with psychiatric disorders as our own responsibility.

– If we remember how people persecuted on grounds of race, religion and politics and threatened with certain death often stood before the closed borders with other countries, we shall not close the door today on those who are genuinely persecuted and seek protection with us.

– If we reflect on the penalties for free thinking under the dictatorship, we will protect the freedom of every idea and every criticism, however much it may be directed against ourselves.

We Germans are one people and one nation. We feel that we belong together because we have lived through the same past. Reconciliation that transcends boundaries cannot be provided by a walled Europe but only by a continent that removes the divisive elements from its borders. We are confident that 8 May is not the last date in the common history of all Germans.

'Let Europe be a family of nations . . .
relishing our national identity no less
than our common European endeavour

Margaret Thatcher

(b. 1925)

THE BRITISH PRIME MINISTER SETS FORTH HER VISION OF EUROPE;
BRUGES, 20 SEPTEMBER 1988

'Let Europe be a family of nations . . . relishing our national identity no less than our common European endeavour'

European integration accelerated during the 1980s and the goal of 'an ever closer union' enshrined in the Treaties of Rome acquired closer definition. Six countries had joined the European Economic Community, established under the original 1957 treaties. By 1988, 12 member states belonged to an organization which had dropped the word 'economic' from its title and was evolving towards the European Union. The aspiration to remove national barriers to trade under the Single European Act (1986) met with approval in Britain, whose population habitually referred to the Community as the 'Common Market'. European Economic and Monetary Union (EMU), however, was a very different matter.

In the summer of 1988 a committee chaired by Jacques Delors, president of the European Commission, was working on plans to introduce a single currency and establish a central bank. Many British Conservatives, taking their cue from the premier's attitudes, protested that the sovereignty of the Westminster parliament, and thereby the country's independence, would be diminished were these innovations to apply to Britain. 'Thatcherism' maintained that the accretion of power by European institutions was a relentless and one-way process, and that its unacknowledged aim was the creation of a federal super-state. The speech led to 'Euro-scepticism' becoming respectable in Britain rather than merely dissident, and hostility to 'European federalism' shaped the consequent public debate.

Thatcher's broad brush portrayed a European 'political class' which was sceptical of capitalism and credulous about government compared to a British political tradition whose devotion to individual freedom and enterprise was more resilient. These convictions reflected her enthusiasm for entrepreneurial values, and Thatcher's flagship policy of privatizing

MARGARET THATCHER (b. 1925)

1946 Graduates in Natural Sciences from University of Oxford.

1953 Called to the Bar of England and Wales.

1959 Elected MP (Conservative) for Finchley.

1970–4 Education Secretary.

1972 Britain's Conservative government signs the Treaty of Accession to the European Economic Community.

Feb 1974 Conservatives lose the general election and are also defeated in the subsequent (Oct) election.

1975 Elected Conservative Party leader.

1979 Forms a government following general-election victory; re-elected in 1983 and 1987.

Nov 1990 Resigns the premiership, unwillingly, and becomes increasingly critical of her successor, John Major.

1990 Awarded Order of Merit.

1992 Resigns as MP, becomes Baroness Thatcher of Kesteven.

1995 Installed as Lady of the Garter, Britain's most ancient chivalric order.

nationalized industries impelled the British economy towards deregulation, greater competition and convergence with American business practice. The speech urges European governments to pay more towards NATO defence costs, as the US had been urging, and the claim that North America is also 'Europe', because of some migrants' origins, is enjoyably mischievous.

This undiplomatic offensive is suffused with Thatcher's suspicion of consensus – in this case that of a European leadership typified as arid, parochial and backward-looking – and the Community is summoned to wider horizons. That international perspective, however, is dominated by the Atlanticist attitudes of Britain and the US, countries which are presented as exemplary in their political wisdom and economic virtue.

Britain's opt-out clauses agreed under the Maastricht Treaty (1992) preserved the pound sterling and the Bank of England, but by then Thatcher had been rejected by a Conservative Party which feared her 'divisiveness'. Europe was central to that drama. In the summer of 1989 Nigel Lawson, as chancellor, and Geoffrey Howe, then foreign secretary, forced an isolated Thatcher to agree in principle to Britain joining the Exchange Rate Mechanism, the Single Currency's designed precursor. Howe resigned from the government in November 1990 and attacked her European convictions as one aspect of a persistent failure to consult her colleagues. Later that month the Cabinet forced her resignation. The strenuous individualism which is lauded in this speech and which marked its delivery had both made, and unmade, Margaret Thatcher's career.

Europe is not the creation of the Treaty of Rome. Nor is the European idea the property of any group or institution. We British are as much heirs to the legacy of European culture as any other nation . . . We in Britain are rightly proud of the way in which, since Magna Carta in the year 1215, we have pioneered and developed representative institutions to stand as bastions of freedom . . . But we know that without the European legacy of political ideas we could not have achieved as much as we did. From classical and medieval thought we have borrowed that concept of the rule of law which marks out a civilized society from barbarism.

'Europe is not the creation of the Treaty of Rome'

But we British have in a very special way contributed to Europe. Over the centuries we have fought to prevent Europe from falling under the dominance of a single power . . . Had it not been for that willingness to fight and to die, Europe would have been united long before now – but not in liberty, not in justice . . .

The European Community is one manifestation of European identity, but it is not the only one. We must never forget that east of the Iron Curtain, people who once enjoyed a full share of European culture, freedom and identity have been cut off from their roots . . .

*'Let Europe be a family of nations . . . relishing our national identity no
less than our common European endeavour'*

Nor should we forget that European values have helped to make the United States of
America into the valiant defender of freedom which she has become . . .

British involvement in Europe . . . is as valid and strong as ever. Yes, we have looked to
wider horizons – as have others – and thank goodness for that because Europe never
would have prospered and never will prosper as a narrow-minded, inward-looking club.

The European Community belongs to all its members. It must reflect the traditions and
aspirations of all its members. Britain does not dream of some cosy, isolated existence on
the fringes . . . Our destiny is in Europe, as part of the Community. This is not to say that
our future lies only in Europe, but nor does that of France or Spain or, indeed, of any
other member.

'Europe . . . never will prosper as a narrow-minded, inward-looking club'

The Community is not an end in itself. Nor is it an institutional device to be constantly
modified according to the dictates of some abstract intellectual concept. Nor must it be
ossified by endless regulation. The European Community is a practical means by which
Europe can ensure the future prosperity and security of its people in a world in which
there are many other powerful nations and groups of nations . . .

Willing and active cooperation between independent sovereign states is the best way to
build a successful European Community. To try to suppress nationhood and concentrate
power at the centre of a European conglomerate would be highly damaging . . . Europe
will be stronger precisely because it has France as France, Spain as Spain, Britain as
Britain, each with its own customs, traditions and identity. It would be folly to try to fit
them into some sort of identikit European personality . . .

Working together more closely does not require power to be centralized in Brussels or
decisions to be taken by an appointed bureaucracy. We have not successfully rolled back
the frontiers of the state in Britain, only to see them re-imposed at a European level with
a European super-state exercising a new dominance from Brussels . . . The Treaty of
Rome itself was intended as a Charter for Economic Liberty. But that is not how it has
always been read, still less applied. The lesson of the economic history of Europe in the
70s and 80s is that central planning and detailed control do not work and that personal
endeavour and initiative do.

By getting rid of barriers, by making it possible for companies to operate on a European
scale, we can best compete with the United States, Japan and other new economic
powers emerging in Asia and elsewhere. And that means action to free markets, action
to widen choice, action to reduce government intervention . . .

The key issue is not whether there should be a European Central Bank. The immediate and practical requirements are:

– to implement the Community's commitment to free movement of capital – in Britain, we have it;

– the abolition through the Community of exchange controls – in Britain, we abolished them in 1979;

– to establish a genuinely free market in financial services in banking, insurance, investment . . .

'Willing and active cooperation between independent sovereign states is the best way to build a successful European Community'

It would be a betrayal if, while breaking down constraints on trade within Europe, the Community were to erect greater external protection . . .

We have a responsibility . . . towards the less developed countries. They need not only aid; more than anything, they need improved trading opportunities if they are to gain the dignity of growing economic strength and independence . . .

The fact is things are going our way: the democratic model of a free-enterprise society has proved itself superior; freedom is on the offensive, a peaceful offensive the world over, for the first time in my lifetime.

We must strive to maintain the United States' commitment to Europe's defence. And that means recognizing the burden on their resources of the world role they undertake and their point that their allies should bear the full part of the defence of freedom, particularly as Europe grows wealthier . . . It is not an institutional problem. It is not a problem of drafting. It is something at once simpler and more profound: it is a question of political will and political courage, of convincing people in all our countries that we cannot rely for ever on others for our defence . . .

Let Europe be a family of nations, understanding each other better, appreciating each other more, doing more together but relishing our national identity no less than our common European endeavour. Let us have a Europe which plays its full part in the wider world, which looks outward not inward, and which preserves that Atlantic community – that Europe on both sides of the Atlantic – which is our noblest inheritance and our greatest strength.

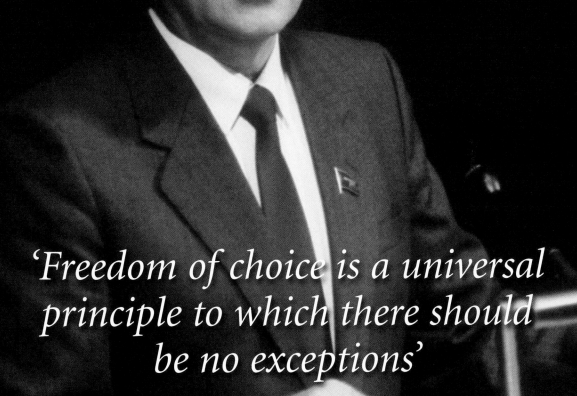

'*Freedom of choice is a universal principle to which there should be no exceptions*'

Mikhail Gorbachev

(b. 1925)

THE SOVIET LEADER ADDRESSES THE GENERAL ASSEMBLY OF THE UNITED NATIONS;
NEW YORK, 7 DECEMBER 1988

Traces of Marxist-Leninist vocabulary could still be heard when Mikhail Gorbachev spoke in public. His rise through the Soviet Communist hierarchy had after all obliged him to espouse an official state doctrine which maintained that individuals' beliefs reflected their socio-economic 'interests', and that the consequent 'contradictions' were therefore 'objectively conditioned'. But these old categories of thought were now submerged within a wider programme of *glasnost* (openness) and *perestroika* (restructuring), which subverted practically everything the USSR had stood for ever since its establishment in 1922.

Gorbachev's conversion to democratization and free-market reforms meant that he was a new version of 'Soviet Man'. By the end of 1988 new laws allowed private ownership of businesses, and preparations were being made for the following year's multi-party elections. Foreign-policy changes reflected the USSR's inability to match US levels of defence spending, and Gorbachev hoped that a reduction in the arms budget would relieve the pressures on the Soviet economy. In December 1987 he therefore signed the Intermediate-Range Nuclear Forces Treaty (INF) with the US, which would eliminate the two countries' ground-launched ballistic and cruise missiles, both nuclear and conventional. This left the US and NATO with a strategic superiority over the USSR in respect of other nuclear weaponry. But the USSR's advantage in conventional weapons remained immense, and Gorbachev's announcement at the UN of a reduction in their numbers, along with a withdrawal of some forces from Eastern Europe and a deep cut in the number of Soviet soldiers, constituted an immense concession. The year 1988 also saw the start of the Soviet withdrawal from Afghanistan, where, following a 1979 invasion and subsequent occupation

MIKHAIL GORBACHEV (b. 1931)

1950–3 Studies at Moscow University.

1953 Joins Communist Party of the Soviet Union (CPSU).

1970 Appointed first secretary for the Stavropol region, northern Caucasus.

1971 Joins CPSU Central Committee.

1978 Appointed secretary of agriculture in Central Committee.

1980–91 Member of the Politburo.

1985–91 General secretary of CPSU.

April 1986 Chernobyl nuclear reactor explosion shows Soviet technological obsolescence.

March–April 1989 Democratic elections held for the Congress of People's Deputies.

1990–1 President of the Soviet Union.

1990 Awarded Nobel Peace Prize.

Aug 1991 Abortive coup attempts to stop USSR's dissolution.

25 Dec 1991 Resigns presidency.

*'Freedom of choice is a universal principle to which
there should be no exceptions'*

in support of a Marxist regime, the USSR had become mired in a war waged by *mujahidin*
'freedom fighters'.

By refusing to lend Soviet support to the beleaguered government of the GDR (East
Germany) Gorbachev ensured its swift collapse in November 1989, and the ensuing year of
democratic revolutions witnessed the overthrow of communist regimes right across Central
and Eastern Europe. The fast pace of change exhilarated Gorbachev's admirers, but in the
short term his reforms aggravated the Soviet economic crisis rather than solving it. His
speech notes resistance in 'certain influential circles', and these included internal critics
who thought the reforms had diminished Soviet prestige and would lead to the USSR's
dissolution. Gorbachev's ambition was for a new federal structure which would contain
Russia and the other nationalities within a continuing union, and he was notably resistant
to the independence of the Baltic states of Estonia, Latvia and Lithuania. But by 1991 he
had been overtaken by events. Soviet reactionaries, hoping to preserve the old-style USSR,
launched a putsch in August and detained the president at his dacha. The coup failed but
Gorbachev's authority was diminished. By the time of his December resignation the ex-USSR
had become the Commonwealth of Independent States, with the Russian Federation as just
one among eleven autonomous countries. Gorbachev's UN address convinced the world
community that a new era had started in the history of international relations, but by 2008
his earlier optimism had faded: 'We had ten years after the Cold War to build a new world
order, and yet we squandered them.'

'Two great revolutions, the French Revolution of 1789 and the Russian Revolution of
1917, have exerted a powerful influence on the actual nature of the historical process . . .
That is a very great spiritual wealth, but . . . it is necessary to seek different roads towards
the future . . . Today we have entered an era when progress will be based on the interests
of all mankind . . .

The history of the past centuries and millennia has been a history of almost ubiquitous
wars . . . They occurred in the clash of social and political interests and national hostility,
be it from ideological or religious incompatibility . . . However, parallel with the process
of wars . . . another process, just as objectively conditioned, was in motion and gaining
force: the process of the emergence of a mutually connected and integral world.

'Force and the threat of force can no longer be, and should not be, instruments of foreign policy'

Further world progress is now possible only through the search for a consensus of all
mankind, in movement towards a new world order . . . The formula of development 'at
another's expense' is becoming outdated. In light of present realities, genuine progress by

infringing upon the rights and liberties of man and peoples, or at the expense of nature, is impossible . . . Behind differences in social structure, in way of life, and in the preference for certain values, stand interests. There is no getting away from that, but neither is there any getting away from the need to find a balance of interests within an international framework . . . It is evident that force and the threat of force can no longer be, and should not be, instruments of foreign policy . . .

Freedom of choice is a universal principle to which there should be no exceptions . . . The variety of socio-political structures which has grown over the last decades . . . presupposes respect for other people's views, tolerance, a preparedness to see phenomena that are different as not necessarily bad or hostile . . .

The de-ideologization of interstate relations has become a demand of the new stage. We are not giving up our convictions, philosophy or traditions . . . Yet we are not going to shut ourselves up within the range of our values . . . Each should prove the advantages of his own system, his own way of life and values, but not through words or propaganda alone, but through real deeds as well. That is, indeed, an honest struggle of ideology, but it must not be carried over into mutual relations between states. Otherwise we simply will not be able to solve a single world problem; arrange broad, mutually advantageous and equitable cooperation between peoples; manage rationally the achievements of the scientific and technical revolution; transform world economic relations; protect the environment; overcome underdevelopment; or put an end to hunger, disease, illiteracy and other mass ills. Finally, in that case, we will not manage to eliminate the nuclear threat and militarism . . .

We must search jointly for a way to achieve the supremacy of the common human idea over the countless multiplicity of centrifugal forces, to preserve the vitality of civilization . . .

Our country is undergoing a truly revolutionary upsurge . . . In order to involve society in implementing the plans for restructuring, it had to be made more truly democratic. Under the badge of democratization, restructuring has now encompassed politics, the economy, spiritual life and ideology . . . We completed the first stage of the process of political reform with the recent decisions by the USSR Supreme Soviet on amendments to the Constitution and the adoption of the Law on Elections. Without stopping, we embarked upon the second stage of this, at which the most important task will be working on the interaction between the central government and the republics . . . and reorganizing the power of the Soviets locally . . .

Soviet democracy is to acquire a firm, normative base. This means such acts as the Law on Freedom of Conscience, on *glasnost*, on public associations and organizations, and on much else. There are now no people in places of imprisonment in the country who have been sentenced for their political or religious convictions . . .

Today I can inform you of the following: the Soviet Union has made a decision on reducing its armed forces. In the next two years, their numerical strength will be reduced by 500,000 persons, and the volume of conventional arms will also be cut considerably. These reductions will be made on a unilateral basis ... By agreement with our allies in the Warsaw Pact, we have made the decision to withdraw six tank divisions from the GDR, Czechoslovakia and Hungary, and to disband them by 1991 ... The Soviet forces situated in those countries will be cut by 50,000 persons, and their arms by 5000 tanks. All remaining Soviet divisions on the territory of our allies will be reorganized. They will be given a different structure from today's which will become unambiguously defensive ...

Relations between the Soviet Union and the United States span 5½ decades ... For too long they were built under the banner of confrontation ... The USSR and the United States created the biggest nuclear missile arsenals, but after objectively recognizing their responsibility, they were able to be the first to conclude an agreement on the reduction and physical destruction of a proportion of these weapons, which threatened both themselves and everyone else. Both sides possess the biggest and the most refined military secrets. But it is they who have laid the basis for, and are developing a system of, mutual verification with regard to both the destruction and the limiting and banning of armaments production ... We are talking first and foremost about consistent progress towards concluding a treaty on a 50 per cent reduction in strategic offensive weapons ... ; about elaborating a convention on the elimination of chemical weapons ... ; and about talks on reducing conventional weapons and armed forces in Europe ...

'The Soviet Union has made a decision on reducing its armed forces'

The movement towards a nuclear-free and non-violent world is capable of fundamentally transforming the political and spiritual face of the planet, but only the very first steps have been taken. Moreover, in certain influential circles, they have been greeted with mistrust and are meeting resistance ... Profound contradictions and the roots of many conflicts have not disappeared. The fact remains that the formation of the peaceful period will take place in conditions of the existence and rivalry of various socio-economic and political systems. However, the meaning of our international efforts, and one of the key tenets of the new thinking, is precisely to impart to this rivalry the quality of sensible competition in conditions of respect for freedom of choice and a balance of interests.

negotiations which followed from 1990 to 1994 were nonetheless often fraught. Following the massacre in the Boipatong township in June 1992, when Zulus killed over 40 people, Mandela suspended negotiations with the government and blamed it, wrongly, for being implicated in the slaughter. The revelation of a far-right plot to derail South Africa's transition to a multi-party democracy – a conspiracy which claimed the life of the ANC's Chris Hani – concentrated minds and the parties resumed their talks on the way ahead. Following the general election of 1994 Mandela formed a 'government of national unity', which included representatives of all ethnic groups and in which F.W. de Klerk, formerly the state president, served as a vice president.

The ANC was now a party of government and had abandoned its earlier commitment to socialism, but labour disputes and high levels of violence still kept foreign investors away. South Africa remained a country scarred by the isolation and divisiveness which had been apartheid's explicit aim, but the compelling personality of its president showed how bitterness could be healed through forgiveness and by the provision of common purpose. As president, Mandela established the Truth and Reconciliation Commission in order to investigate human-rights abuses in as non-partisan a way as possible. He also understood how important symbolic actions could be in the business of building a nation, and when South Africa hosted the Rugby World Cup in 1995, he encouraged the whole country to support the Springboks – the national side whose mostly white faces had once made them an intrinsic part of the old supremacy's sporting establishment. The Springboks won the tournament and the widespread local enthusiasm for the victory showed that a South African multiracial renaissance was a genuine possibility. Mandela's grace could also take a highly personal form. Dr Percy Yutar, the state prosecutor in the trial which had condemned him to life imprisonment in 1964, was invited by Mandela to lunch in the presidential palace and told that he had only been doing his job. It was a characteristic touch.

Today, all of us do, by our presence here, and by our celebrations in other parts of our country and the world, confer glory and hope to newborn liberty.

Out of the experience of an extraordinary human disaster that lasted too long must be born a society of which all humanity will be proud.

Our daily deeds as ordinary South Africans must produce an actual South African reality that will reinforce humanity's belief in justice, strengthen its confidence in the nobility of the human soul and sustain all our hopes for a glorious life for all.

'Out of the experience of an extraordinary human disaster that lasted too long must be born a society of which all humanity will be proud'

All this we owe both to ourselves and to the peoples of the world who are so well represented here today.

To my compatriots, I have no hesitation in saying that each one of us is as intimately attached to the soil of this beautiful country as are the famous jacaranda trees of Pretoria and the mimosa trees of the bushveld.

Each time one of us touches the soil of this land, we feel a sense of personal renewal. The national mood changes as the seasons change.

We are moved by a sense of joy and exhilaration when the grass turns green and the flowers bloom.

That spiritual and physical oneness we all share with this common homeland explains the depth of the pain we all carried in our hearts as we saw our country tear itself apart in a terrible conflict, and as we saw it spurned, outlawed and isolated by the peoples of the world, precisely because it has become the universal base of the pernicious ideology and practice of racism and racial oppression.

We, the people of South Africa, feel fulfilled that humanity has taken us back into its bosom, that we, who were outlaws not so long ago, have today been given the rare privilege to be host to the nations of the world on our own soil.

'Each time one of us touches the soil of this land, we feel a sense of personal renewal'

We thank all our distinguished international guests for having come to take possession with the people of our country of what is, after all, a common victory for justice, for peace, for human dignity.

We trust that you will continue to stand by us as we tackle the challenges of building peace, prosperity, non-sexism, non-racialism and democracy.

We deeply appreciate the role that the masses of our people and their political mass democratic, religious, women, youth, business, traditional and other leaders have played to bring about this conclusion. Not least among them is my Second Deputy President, the Honourable F.W. de Klerk.

We would also like to pay tribute to our security forces, in all their ranks, for the distinguished role they have played in securing our first democratic elections and the transition to democracy, from bloodthirsty forces which still refuse to see the light.

The time for the healing of the wounds has come.

The moment to bridge the chasms that divide us has come. The time to build is upon us.

On 31 August 1994 the Irish Republican Army (IRA) announced a cessation of its military operations with effect from midnight. One phase of the 'peace process' had ended and another had begun.

The Sunningdale Agreement of 1973, referred to here by Seamus Heaney, was a British government attempt at solving Northern Ireland's crisis: the local Stormont Assembly, suspended since 1972, was to be revived; the province's executive would be a devolved administration with the Unionist majority agreeing to share power with its local political opponents; Irish government ministers and Dáil representatives would sit alongside members of the Northern Ireland Executive and Assembly in a Council of Ireland. The Unionist leadership initially endorsed the agreement but the Protestant workforce rejected it. A general strike by the Ulster Workers' Council ensured the agreement's demise, and the province collapsed into the cycle of retaliatory Protestant–Catholic violence which had consumed the six counties ever since the onset of the 'Troubles' in 1968. The Downing Street Declaration of 15 December 1993 broke the impasse: the British government stated that it had 'no selfish strategic or economic interest in Northern Ireland' and the government of Éire formally agreed that a united Ireland required the consent of a majority of the Northern Irish electorate.

SEAMUS HEANEY (b. 1939)

1961 Graduates from Queen's University, Belfast.

1965 Publishes his first collection of verse, *Eleven Poems*.

1966–72 Lecturer in English literature, Queen's University, Belfast.

1970–1 Visiting lecturer, University of California, Berkeley.

1975 Publishes *North*.

1980 *Selected Poems 1965–1975*.

1982 Appointed part-time lecturer, Harvard University.

1984 Elected to the Boylston Chair of Rhetoric and Oratory, Harvard University.

1984 *Station Island; Sweeney Astray*, a translation from Middle Irish.

1988 *The Government of the Tongue* (collected essays).

1989–94 Professor of Poetry, University of Oxford.

1990 *New Selected Poems 1966–1987*.

1991 Publishes *The Cure at Troy*: a version of Sophocles' *Philoctetes*, and his verse collection *Seeing Things*.

1995 *The Redress of Poetry* (collected essays).

1995 Awarded Nobel Prize for Literature.

1998 *Opened Ground: Poems,1966–1996*.

1999 *Beowulf: A New Translation*.

'The Ireland I now inhabit is one that these
Irish contemporaries have helped to imagine'

Heaney was right in thinking that a quarter century of 'hardening attitudes' was ending, but further progress remained tortuous. The Good Friday Agreement (10 April 1998) set the terms for a devolved and inclusive government, along with troop reductions and civil rights for the province's Catholic population. An elected Northern Ireland Assembly and a power-sharing executive came into being, with Unionists agreeing to work with the Irish republican Sinn Féin – a party with close IRA links. Continuing Unionist suspicions focused on the IRA's retention of weaponry, and the devolved arrangements were suspended between 2002 and 2007. In 2005 the IRA embarked on a complete decommissioning of its arsenal – a process overseen by an international commission. The reconciled leadership of Sinn Féin and of the Democratic Unionist Party formed a joint administration in 2007 and, following that year's elections, the Assembly reconvened. 'Operation Banner', the British army's operation in Northern Ireland, came to an end and the province was at peace.

In this speech Heaney traces the connection between his own imaginative evolution and the often tragic dimension to Ireland's politics. The heavily stressed lines of his verse in *North* communicate the tension of 1970s Ireland, and poetry's linguistic ability to heal constriction and transcend division has been a constant Heaney preoccupation. Born to a Catholic family in the rural North, he has found themes of epic significance in the region's landscape and its people's endurance, while the influence of both Anglo-Saxon and Irish-language literature on his poetry accounts for its distinctively 'northern' idiom. The straightening up that he described in Stockholm includes a poetic shift towards the spacious and lyrical, with *Station Island* showing Dante's influence and *Seeing Things* absorbing echoes of Virgil. His journey into 'the wideness of language' continues to transformative effect.

In the 1940s, when I was the eldest child of an ever-growing family in rural Co. Derry, we crowded together in the three rooms of a traditional thatched farmstead and lived a kind of den-life which was more or less emotionally and intellectually proofed against the outside world . . . When a wind stirred in the beeches, it also stirred an aerial wire attached to the topmost branch of the chestnut tree. Down it swept . . . right on into the innards of our wireless set where a little pandemonium of burbles and squeaks would suddenly give way to the voice of a BBC newsreader . . . We could pick up . . . the names of bombers and of cities bombed, of war fronts and army divisions . . . of casualties suffered and advances made. But even so, none of the news of these world-spasms entered me as terror . . . The wartime, in other words, was pre-reflective time for me . . .

Then as the years went on and my listening became more deliberate, I would climb up on an arm of our big sofa to get my ear closer to the wireless speaker . . . and in that intent proximity to the dial I grew familiar with the names of foreign stations . . . I had already begun a journey into the wideness of the world beyond. This in turn became a journey into the wideness of language . . . I credit poetry for making this space-walk possible. I credit poetry . . . for making possible a fluid and restorative relationship between the mind's centre and its circumference, between the child gazing at the word 'Stockholm' on the face of the radio dial and the man facing the faces that he meets in Stockholm at this most privileged moment . . .

I found myself in the mid-1970s in another small house. This time in Co. Wicklow south of Dublin, with a young family of my own and a slightly less imposing radio set, listening to the rain in the trees and to the news of bombings closer to home – not only those by the Provisional IRA in Belfast but equally atrocious assaults in Dublin by loyalist paramilitaries . . .

There are times . . . when we want the poem to be not only pleasurably right but also compellingly wise, not only a surprising variation played upon the world, but a retuning of the world itself . . . This is the want I was experiencing . . . in Co. Wicklow . . .

'There are times . . . when we want the poem to be not only pleasurably right but also compellingly wise'

Until the British government caved in to the strong-arm tactics of the Ulster loyalist workers after the Sunningdale Conference in 1974, a well-disposed mind could still hope to make sense of the circumstances, to balance what was promising with what was destructive . . . For the 20 long years between then and the ceasefires of August 1994, such a hope proved impossible. The violence from below was productive of nothing but a retaliatory violence from above . . . and people settled in to a quarter century of . . . hardening attitudes and narrowing possibilities that were the natural result of political solidarity, traumatic suffering and sheer emotional self-protectiveness . . .

'People settled in to a quarter century of . . . hardening attitudes and narrowing possibilities'

It is difficult at times to repress the thought that history is about as instructive as an abbatoir . . . Which is why for years I was bowed to the desk like some monk bowed over his prie-dieu, some dutiful contemplative . . . constrained by his obedience to his rule to repeat the effort and the posture. Blowing up sparks for meagre heat. Forgetting faith, straining towards good works . . .

Then finally and happily . . . I straightened up. I began a few years ago to try to make space in my reckoning and imagining for the marvellous as well as for the murderous . . .

The century has witnessed the defeat of Nazism by force of arms; but the erosion of the Soviet regimes was caused, among other things, by the sheer persistence, beneath the imposed ideological conformity, of cultural values . . . The way in which walls have come

'The Ireland I now inhabit is one that these
Irish contemporaries have helped to imagine'

down in Europe . . . inspires a hope that new possibility can still open up in Ireland as well . . .

When the poet W.B. Yeats stood on this platform more than 70 years ago, Ireland was emerging from the throes of a traumatic civil war . . . Yeats barely alluded to the civil war in his Nobel speech . . . He came to Sweden to tell the world that the local works of poets and dramatists had been as important to the transformation of his native place and times as the ambushes of guerrilla armies; and his boast in that elevated prose was essentially the same as the one he would make . . . in his poem 'The Municipal Gallery Revisited'. There Yeats presents himself among the portraits and heroic narrative paintings which celebrate the events and personalities of recent history and all of a sudden realizes that something truly epoch-making has occurred:

> "This is not," I say,
> "The dead Ireland of my youth, but an Ireland
> The poets have imagined, terrible and gay."

And the poem concludes . . . :

> Think where man's glory most begins and ends,
> And say my glory was I had such friends.

. . . I ask you to do what Yeats asked his audience to do and think of the achievement of Irish poets and dramatists and novelists over the past 40 years, among whom I am proud to count great friends . . . The Ireland I now inhabit is one that these Irish contemporaries have helped to imagine . . .

When the bard Demodocus sings of the fall of Troy and of the slaughter that accompanied it, Odysseus weeps and Homer says that his tears were like the tears of a wife on a battlefield weeping for the death of a fallen husband:

> At the sight of the man panting and dying there,
> she slips down to enfold him, crying out;
> then feels the spears, prodding her back and shoulders,
> and goes bound into slavery and grief.
> Piteous weeping wears away her cheeks:
> but no more piteous than Odysseus' tears,
> cloaked as they were, now, from the company.

. . . The callousness of those spear shafts on the woman's back and shoulders survives time and translation . . . But there is another kind of adequacy which is specific to lyric poetry . . . It has to do . . . with the buoyancy generated by cadence and tone and rhyme and stanza . . . It is this which keeps the poet's ear straining to hear the totally persuasive voice behind all the other informing voices. Which is a way of saying that I have never quite climbed down from the arm of that sofa.

'Socialism or death!'

Fidel Castro

(b. 1926)

CUBA'S LEADER SPEAKS ON THE OCCASION OF THE 40TH ANNIVERSARY
OF HIS COUNTRY'S SOCIALIST REVOLUTION; SANTIAGO DE CUBA,
1 JANUARY 1999

The regular delivery of speeches lasting several hours was one of the methods used by Fidel Castro in order to maintain high levels of revolutionary consciousness among Cuba's population and thereby to keep his grip on power. A Castro oration was never an event for the faint-hearted, and his audiences needed to be possessed of physical stamina as well as ideological rectitude.

His commemoration of the Cuban revolution's 40th anniversary showed that Castro, then in his 73rd year, could still combine Marxist doctrine with nationalist sentiment to potent effect, and the speech exemplifies some of his most characteristic certitudes. Cuba's revolutionary narrative merges with world historical trends, and Castro's urgent delineation of that process involves his listeners in a continuing struggle – one whose global victory is assured but whose successful resolution nonetheless requires their lasting commitment. Castro is speaking in the city where he first proclaimed victory for the revolution, and there is a theatrical quality to his re-creation of past emotions. He evokes the revolutionaries' nostalgia for the intensity of guerrilla solidarity, and their success is attributed to the force of ideas as well as cleverness in strategy. The revolution, in Castro's dramatic rendition, acquires its own secular liturgy: the sacrifices of the dead are remembered with gratitude and thanks are given for past victories. Financial markets' instability anticipates capitalism's collapse – and the world's subsequent salvation through socialism.

Castro's conviction of his own destiny was obvious right from the start of Cuba's revolution. At his trial in 1953, following the failure of an attack on the Moncada Barracks in Santiago de Cuba, he told the court: 'I warn you. I am just beginning . . . Condemn me. It does not matter. History will absolve me.' Once freed from prison, Castro formed the 26th of July Movement which, named after the day of that attack, organized the military struggle to overthrow President Fulgencia Batista, whose pro-American regime was closely associated with the Cuban elite's business interests.

FIDEL CASTRO (b. 1926)

1953 Sentenced to 15 years' imprisonment for participation in an attack (26 July) on Moncada Barracks, Santiago de Cuba; released under a general amnesty in 1955.

Dec 1956 Returns from Mexico to lead guerrilla warfare against the Cuban army.

1 Jan 1959 Proclaims victory of the Cuban revolution from a balcony on Santiago de Cuba's city hall; sworn in as premier (16 Feb).

1965 First secretary, Communist Party of Cuba.

1976 Becomes president of the Council of State (president of Cuba), and president of the Council of Ministers, following abolition of the office of premier.

Feb 2008 Resigns presidential offices and title of 'commander-in-chief' of Cuban armed forces.

The guerrilla army that Castro led to victory barely numbered 300 partisans, and his emphasis on the 'enormous difference in equipment and strength between the enemy and us' was no idle boast. He gained power as a nationalist resentful of US influence on Cuba, and the asceticism of Castro's revolutionary style was in conscious contrast to the lush decadence of Batista's corrupt government. Large-scale expropriation of Cuban property owned by US corporations, as well as agrarian reforms limiting individual land-ownership, placed the new Cuban regime on the extreme left, and the adoption of state socialism resulted in the emigration to the US of some one million Cubans whose many pressure groups became the fulcrum of the anti-Castro opposition. In December 1961 Castro officially declared himself to be a Marxist–Leninist and announced that Cuba would be ruled as a communist state. Two months later the US announced the imposition of a financial and commercial embargo on Cuba, a state which was now firmly allied with the USSR politically, economically and militarily. The 'special period', as Castro liked to call it, had started.

'

I am trying to recall that night of 1 January 1959; I am reliving and perceiving impressions and details as if everything were occurring at this very moment . . .

Our fleeting sadness at the moment of victory was nostalgia for the experiences we had lived through . . . We had to abandon our mountains, our rural life, our habits of absolute and obligatory austerity, our tense life of constant vigilance in the face of an enemy that could appear by land or air at any moment: a healthy, hard, pure life and one of great sacrifices and shared dangers, in which men become brothers and their best virtues flourish . . .

The enormous difference in equipment and strength between the enemy and us forced us to do the impossible . . . The infallible tactic of attacking the enemy when it was on the move was a key factor. The art of provoking those forces into moving out of their well-fortified and generally invulnerable positions became one of our commands' greatest skills . . . What we learned in the mountains and dense forest areas was applied in the lowland areas . . . The same method wound up being applied within the cities . . . That was how the plan was conceived to attack and take control of the garrison in the Santiago de Cuba plaza . . .

'Honour and eternal glory, infinite respect and affection to those that died to make possible the country's definitive independence'

Honour and eternal glory, infinite respect and affection to those that died to make possible the country's definitive independence: for all those who wrote that epic in the mountains, the plains and cities; to the underground guerrillas and fighters; to those who, after the triumph, died in other glorious missions or loyally gave up their youth and energies to the cause of justice, sovereignty and the redemption of their people . . .

The people of yesterday, illiterate and semi-literate, and with only a minimal political awareness, were capable of making the revolution, of defending the nation, of subsequently achieving an exceptional political consciousness and initiating a revolutionary process that is unparalleled in this hemisphere and in the world . . .

'Our eternal people have resisted 40 years of aggression, blockade, and economic, political and ideological warfare'

With the participation of three generations, our heroic people of yesterday and today, our eternal people have resisted 40 years of aggression, blockade, and economic, political and ideological warfare waged by the strongest and richest imperial power that has ever existed in the history of the world. The most extraordinary page of glory . . . has been written during these years of the special period, when we were left absolutely alone . . . 90 miles from the United States, and we decided to carry on.

Our people aren't any better than other peoples. Their historic greatness is derived from the singular fact of having been put to the test and having been able to withstand it. It's not a great people in and of itself; but rather a people which has made itself great, and its capacity to do so is born out of the greatness of the ideas and the righteousness of the causes it defends. There are no other causes like these, and there never have been . . .

The struggle begun on 1 January 1959 has inexorably turned into a struggle . . . for the interests of all humanity . . . But the solutions for humanity will not come from the good will of those who rule and exploit the world . . . The current system is unsustainable because it is based on blind and chaotic laws which are ruinous and destructive to society and nature . . . The most fanatical defenders of and believers in the market have converted it into a new religion. This is how the theology of the market emerged . . . Out of respect for the genuine religions practised honestly by billions of people throughout the world and out of respect for the genuine theologians, we could simply add that the theology of the market is sectarian, fundamentalist and not ecumenical . . .

'The most fanatical defenders of and believers in the market have converted it into a new religion'

New and unsuspected phenomena are emerging, ones which escape the control of governments and international financial institutions . . . The slightest carelessness can lead speculators to attack, devaluing the currency and liquidating hard currency reserves, built up over decades, in a matter of days . . . Absolutely no one is or can be safe. The wolves, grouped in packs and aided by computer programs, know where to attack, when to attack and why to attack . . .

The prevailing order flip-flops between inflation, recession, deflation, potential overproduction crises, and sustained slumps of basic products . . .

Economic crises and the absence of solutions within the established international economic system will destabilize many governments. We are living through a stage in which events move more quickly than consciousness of the realities under which we suffer. We must sow ideas and unmask deceit, sophism and hypocrisy, using methods and means which counteract the disinformation and institutionalized lies . . .

'May there be an end to the tyranny of an order that imposes blind, anarchic and chaotic principles'

May there be an end to the tyranny of an order that imposes blind, anarchic and chaotic principles, that is leading the human species towards the abyss . . .

The unfathomable differences between rich and poor within each country and between countries cannot continue growing. They must progressively diminish until they disappear. May merit, capacity, creative spirit, and what each individual actually contributes to the welfare of humanity, as opposed to theft, speculation and the exploitation of the weakest, determine differences. May humanism be genuinely practised, with concrete actions and not hypocritical slogans . . .

To all of our compatriots, and especially the young, I assure you that the next 40 years will be decisive for the world. Before you there are tasks that are incomparably more complex and difficult. New glorious goals await you; the honour of being Cuban revolutionaries demands it . . . In the ideological war, as in armed battles, there are casualties . . . I was recalling today that in the midst of the war . . . of all the young volunteers . . . one in ten was able to withstand it, but that one was worth ten, a hundred, a thousand. By strengthening awareness, forming character, educating the young in the difficult school of life in our era, sowing solid ideas, using arguments that are irrefutable, preaching through example and trusting in the honour of mankind, we can ensure that for every ten, nine remain in their battle posts alongside the flag, the revolution and the homeland. Socialism or death!

'By putting our money where our heart is . . . we will mould the world into a kinder, more loving shape'

Anita Roddick

(1942–2007)

THE FOUNDER OF THE BODY SHOP ADDRESSES THE INTERNATIONAL FORUM
ON GLOBALIZATION; SEATTLE, 27 NOVEMBER 1999

During the late 20th century socialism was on the retreat both in the West and in large areas of the developing world. During this new phase in the evolution of market capitalism, global trading patterns became increasingly interlinked, and advances in information technology meant that deregulated financial markets could shift massive flows of capital across national boundaries within seconds. 'Globalization' boosted trade, encouraged productivity gains and lowered prices, but critics alleged that it exploited the low-paid, was indifferent to environmental concerns and subjected the Third World to a monopolistic form of capitalism. Many radicals within Western societies who wished to protest against this process joined voluntary bodies, charities and other non-governmental organizations, rather than the marginalized political parties of the left. The environmental movement itself grew out of the recognition that the world was interconnected, and an angry, if diffuse, international coalition of interests emerged. Anita Roddick was its impassioned advocate.

Roddick was an entrepreneur of genius who had pioneered 'ethical consumerism' through the Body Shop, the cosmetics company she had founded and which prohibited the use of animal-tested ingredients in the manufacture of its products. Feminist principle would lead her to castigate the traditional cosmetics industry as 'a monster selling unattainable dreams, one that lies, cheats and exploits women'. Having started as one shop in Brighton, the company became a multinational with some 2000 branches, but despite the dizzying scale of this expansion, Roddick stuck to 'fair trade' principles when dealing with her suppliers in evolving markets. The 'Queen of Green' campaigned against sweat shops and for workers' rights, and the Body Shop's use of locally sourced organic products aimed to support the economic base and cultural diversity of traditional societies. Roddick was a prominent supporter of debt relief for governments struggling to meet the conditions attached to International Monetary Fund and World Bank loans. She had a ready audience among the protesters who in November 1999 gathered in Seattle, where the ministerial

ANITA RODDICK (1942–2007)

1976 Founds Body Shop.

1990 Establishes Children on the Edge, a charity for the disadvantaged in Asia and Eastern Europe; co-founds *The Big Issue*, a magazine sold by the homeless and published on their behalf.

1984 Body Shop becomes a public company.

1990 Establishes Body Shop Foundation, a major donor to charities.

2003 Becomes Dame of the British Empire.

2006 Body Shop bought by L'Oréal, a company involved in animal testing and whose part-owner Nestlé has been criticized for its treatment of Third World producers; Roddick claims that the Body Shop will bring change within L'Oréal.

2007 Makes public that she has been diagnosed as having contracted hepatitis C following a 1971 blood transfusion.

'By putting our money where our heart is . . . we will mould the world into a kinder, more loving shape'

conference of the World Trade Organization (WTO) was about to embark on a new round of international trade negotiations.

WTO officials pointed out that labour conditions and green issues were beyond their remit and that their sole aim was to discourage 'protectionism'. Government subsidies to endangered sectors and tariffs on competing imports were futile and reactionary measures. Economic development would eventually lead to higher-paid work, but in the meantime the only alternative to low-paid jobs in many areas of the Third World was no jobs at all. Roddick was vulnerable to these criticisms, but she was no mere 'New Age' theorist and had shown how business could provide moral leadership while also delivering a profit. Nuances of argument were lost, however, when over 40,000 protesters took to the Seattle streets on 30 November 1999 in a massive and pre-planned programme of civil disturbance which initially overwhelmed the local police and included acts of vandalism by anarchist groups. Order was restored later that day and the conference was able to convene. Negotiations, however, soon collapsed, with emerging economies rivalling older ones in their attachment to protectionist barriers.

We are in Seattle arguing for a world trade system that puts basic human rights and the environment at its core. We have the most powerful corporations of the world ranged against us. They own the media that informs us – or fails to inform us. And they probably own the politicians too. It's enough to make anybody feel a little edgy.

So here's a question for the world trade negotiators. Who is the system you are lavishing so much attention on supposed to serve? We can ask the same question of the gleaming towers of Wall Street or the City of London – and the powerful men and women who tinker with the money system which drives world trade. Who is this system for?

'The great global myth being that the current world trade system is for anything but money'

Let's look more closely. Every day the gleaming towers of high finance oversee a global flow of two trillion dollars . . . And the terrifying thing is that only three per cent of that has anything to do with trade at all. Let alone free trade between equal communities.

It has everything to do with money. The great global myth being that the current world trade system is for anything but money.

The other 97 per cent of the two trillion is speculation. It is froth – but froth with terrifying power over people's lives . . . We all of us, rich and poor, have to live with the insecurity caused by an out-of-control global casino with a built-in bias towards instability. Because it is instability that makes money for the money-traders . . .

I spend much of every year travelling around the world, talking to people in the front line of globalization: women, community farmers, children. I know how unrealistic these myths are. Not just in developing countries but right under our noses.

Like the small farmers of the USA . . . Globalization means that the subsidies go to the big farms, while the small family farms – the heart of so many American communities – go to the wall . . .

We have a world trading system that is blind to this kind of injustice. And as the powers of governments shrink, this system is, in effect, our new unelected, uncontrollable world government. One that outlaws our attempts to make things better . . .

The truth is that the WTO, and the group of unelected trade officials who run it, are now the world's highest court, with the right to overturn local laws and safety regulations wherever they say it 'interferes with trade'.

This is world government by default, but it is a blind government. It looks at the measurements of money, but it can't see anything else. It can recognize profits and losses, but it deliberately turns its face away from human rights, child labour or keeping the environment viable for future generations.

It is government without heart, and without heart you find the creativity of the human spirit starts to dwindle too . . .

The truth is that 'free trade' was originally about the freedom of communities to trade equally with each other. It was never intended to be what it is today. A licence for the big, the powerful and the rich to ride roughshod over the small, the weak and the poor . . .

> *'It is government without heart, and without heart you find the creativity of the human spirit starts to dwindle too'*

Nobody could be more in favour of a global outlook than I am. Internationalism means that we can see into the dark corners of the world, and hold those companies to account when they are devastating forests or employing children as bonded labour. Globalization is the complete opposite, its rules pit country against country and workers against workers in the blinkered pursuit of international competitiveness.

Internationalism means we can link together at local level across the world, and use our power as consumers. Working together, across all sectors, we can turn businesses from private greed to public good. It means, even more important, that we can start understanding each other in a way that no generation has managed before.

'By putting our money where our heart is . . . we will mould the world into a kinder, more loving shape'

Let's be clear about this. It's not trade we're against. It's exploitation and unchecked power . . . Businesses which forego profits to build communities, or keep production local rather than employing semi-slaves in distant sweatshops, risk losing business to cheaper competitors without such commitments, and being targeted for take-over by the slash-and-burn corporate raiders. Reinforced by the weight of the WTO . . .

Business has to be a force for social change. It is not enough to avoid hideous evil – it must, we must, actively do good . . . The rules have got to change. We need a radical alternative that puts people before profit . . . We must start measuring our success differently.

'Let's measure the success of places and corporations against how much they enhance human well-being'

If politicians, businesses and analysts only measure the bottom line – the growth in money – then it's not surprising the world is skewed. It's not surprising that the WTO is half-blind, recognizing slash-and-burn corporations but not the people they destroy. It's not surprising that it values flipping hamburgers . . . as a valuable activity, but takes no account of those other jobs – the caring, educating and loving work that we all know needs doing . . . Let's measure the success of places and corporations against how much they enhance human well-being . . . Measuring what really matters can give us the revolution in kindness we so desperately need. That's the real bottom line.

And finally, we must remember we already have power as consumers and as organizations forming strategic and increasingly influential alliances for change . . . If consumers won't buy, nothing on earth can make them. Just look at how European consumers have forced the biotech industry's back up against the wall.

We have to be political consumers, vigilante consumers. With the barrage of propaganda served up to us every day, we have to be. We must be wise enough so that – whatever they decide at the trade talks – we know where to put our energy and our money. No matter what we're told or cajoled to do, we must work together to get the truth out in cooperation for the best, not competition for the cheapest.

By putting our money where our heart is, refusing to buy the products which exploit, by forming powerful strategic alliances, we will mould the world into a kinder, more loving shape.

Britain's duty to support the US politically and militarily. US intelligence had concluded that the al-Qaeda network, led by Osama bin Laden, was responsible for the atrocity and that the attack had been planned from the organization's bases in Afghanistan, where it was being protected by a government run by the Taliban, an Islamist group. British naval forces were deployed in support of US air strikes launched against the bases five days after this speech's delivery. The Taliban government collapsed during the ensuing land war, in which British troops served alongside the US army, but despite the installation of a democratically elected government in 2004, the military coalition became involved in a prolonged war waged by Taliban guerrilla forces.

Blair's commitment to a morally directed foreign and military policy faced its most extreme test during the war in Iraq from 2003 onwards. President George W. Bush and his advisers had decided that the struggle against terrorism required the removal from power of Saddam Hussein, who, though a brutal president of Iraq and a threat to his neighbours, was not linked to the 9/11 attacks. Britain's military involvement in the campaign divided not just the Labour Party but the entire country. When Blair left office, the kaleidoscope he had described six years earlier remained shaken and the world had resisted his reordering.

'In retrospect, the Millennium marked only a moment in time. It was the events of September 11 that marked a turning point in history, where we confront the dangers of the future and assess the choices facing humankind. It was a tragedy. An act of evil. From this nation goes our deepest sympathy and prayers for the victims and our profound solidarity with the American people. We were with you at the first. We will stay with you to the last . . .

'It was the events of September 11 that marked a turning point in history'

Our way of life is a great deal stronger and will last a great deal longer than the actions of fanatics . . . This is a battle with only one outcome: our victory not theirs . . . Be in no doubt: Bin Laden and his people organized this atrocity. The Taliban aid and abet him. He will not desist from further acts of terror. They will not stop helping him . . .

The action we take will be proportionate; targeted; we will do all we humanly can to avoid civilian casualties. But understand what we are dealing with . . . There is no compromise possible with such people, no meeting of minds, no point of understanding with such terror. Just a choice: defeat it or be defeated by it. And defeat it we must.

Today conflicts rarely stay within national boundaries. Today a tremor in one financial market is repeated in the markets of the world. Today confidence is global; either its presence or its absence . . . I have long believed this interdependence defines the new world we live in. People say: we are only acting because it's the USA that was attacked. Double standards, they say. But when Milosevic embarked on the ethnic cleansing of Muslims in Kosovo, we acted . . . and look what happened, we won, the refugees went home, the policies of ethnic cleansing were reversed . . .

And I tell you if Rwanda happened again as it did in 1993, when a million people were slaughtered in cold blood, we would have a moral duty to act there also . . . The power of the international community could, with our help, sort out the blight that is the continuing conflict in the Democratic Republic of the Congo, where three million people have died through war or famine in the last decade.

'The world community must show as much its capacity for compassion as for force'

A Partnership for Africa, between the developed and developing world, is there to be done if we find the will . . . We could defeat climate change if we chose to . . . With imagination, we could use or find the technologies that create energy without destroying our planet . . . And if we wanted to, we could breathe new life into the Middle East Peace Process and we must . . .

The world community must show as much its capacity for compassion as for force. The critics will say: but how can the world be a community? Nations act in their own self-interest. Of course they do. But what is the lesson of financial markets, climate change, international terrorism, nuclear proliferation or world trade? It is that our self-interest and our mutual interest are today inextricably woven together . . .

The issue is not how to stop globalization. The issue is how we use the power of community to combine it with justice . . . If we follow the principles that have served us so well at home – that power, wealth and opportunity must be in the hands of the many, not the few – if we make that our guiding light for the global economy, then it will be a force for good . . .

'Our self-interest and our mutual interest are today inextricably woven together'

The governing idea of modern social democracy is community. Founded on the principles of social justice. That people should rise according to merit not birth; that the test of any decent society is . . . the commitment to the poor and weak.

But values aren't enough . . . Our policies only succeed when the realism is as clear as the idealism. This party's strength today comes from the journey of change and learning we have made . . . We learnt that equality is about equal worth, not equal outcomes . . . On this journey, the values have never changed . . . But the means do change. The journey hasn't ended. It never ends . . .

When we act to bring to account those that committed the atrocity of September 11, we do so not out of bloodlust. We do so because it is just. We do not act against Islam. The true followers of Islam are our brothers and sisters in this struggle. Bin Laden is no more obedient to the proper teachings of the Koran than those crusaders of the 12th century, who pillaged and murdered, represented the teaching of the Gospel.

'The governing idea of modern social democracy is community'

It is time the West confronted its ignorance of Islam. Jews, Muslims and Christians are all children of Abraham. This is the moment to bring the faiths closer in understanding of our common values and heritage, a source of unity and strength.

It is time also for parts of Islam to confront prejudice against America, and not only Islam but parts of Western societies too. America has its faults as a society, as we have ours . . . But it is a free country, a democracy, it is our ally and some of the reaction to September 11 betrays a hatred of America that shames those that feel it.

So I believe this is a fight for freedom. And I want to make it a fight for justice too. Justice not only to punish the guilty. But justice to bring those same values of democracy and freedom to people round the world. And I mean: freedom, not only in the narrow sense of personal liberty but in the broader sense of each individual having the economic and social freedom to develop their potential to the full. That is what community means, founded on the equal worth of all.

The starving, the wretched, the dispossessed, the ignorant, those living in want and squalor from the deserts of northern Africa to the slums of Gaza, to the mountain ranges of Afghanistan: they too are our cause. This is a moment to seize. The kaleidoscope has been shaken. The pieces are in flux. Soon they will settle again. Before they do, let us reorder this world around us.

'*Whatever the country, freedom of thought and expression are universal human rights*'

Orhan Pamuk

(b.1952)

THE TURKISH NOVELIST DELIVERS THE INAUGURAL PEN ARTHUR MILLER
FREEDOM TO WRITE MEMORIAL LECTURE AT THE WORLD VOICES FESTIVAL;
NEW YORK CITY, 25 APRIL 2006

I n an interview with the Swiss publication *Das Magazin*, published in February 2005, Orhan Pamuk was reported as saying of his native Turkey: 'Thirty thousand Kurds and a million Armenians were killed here. Hardly anyone dares to mention it. And so I do.' These words were used as evidence against him during the cause célèbre which forms the immediate background to this address.

Turkey's new penal code became effective in June 2005 and ultra-nationalist lawyers filed charges against Pamuk citing that legislation's Article 301, whose original wording made it a crime for the country's citizens to 'denigrate Turkishness'. Pamuk's trial started in December 2005, but the charges against him, which carried a penalty of between six months and three years' imprisonment, were dropped. The case involved a retrospective application of the penal code's provisions and, as a result, the Ministry of Justice's approval was required before prosecution could proceed. Mindful of its international reputation, and especially concerned about the progress of its application to join the European Union, the Turkish government refused to allow the case's prosecution.

Pamuk's fiction deals with East–West cultural cross-currents and draws much of its strength from a close observation of Istanbul, a city which straddles the European–Asian boundary. He describes modernity's unsettling impact on an ancient culture and is sensitive to the way in which traditionalist, non-Western societies fear their humiliation by a progressive, self-satisfied West. Public commitment did not come easily to Pamuk , a scrupulous stylist who values his art's detachment and whose pen resists activism's ready-made slogans.

This lecture describes the intellectual tensions of a natural aesthete impelled towards the recognition of difficult truths: writers cannot escape their context, and protest in the face

ORHAN PAMUK (b. 1952)

1976 Graduates from Istanbul University, following an earlier period studying architecture at Istanbul Technical University.

1982 Publishes first novel, *Cevdet Bey ve O ullari* (Cevdet Bey and Sons).

1985–8 Visiting Scholar at Columbia University, New York City.

1985 *Beyaz Kale* (trans. *The White Castle*, 1991) enjoys international success.

1990 *Kara Kitap* (trans. *The Black Book*, 1995).

1998 B*enim Adim Kirmizi* (trans. *My Name is Red*, 2001).

1998 Refuses Turkish government recognition as 'state artist'.

2002 *Kar* (trans. *Snow*, 2005).

2003 *Istanbul: Hatiralar ve Sehir* (trans. *Istanbul: Memories of a City*, 2006).

2006 Appointed Visiting Professor at Columbia University.

2006 Awarded Nobel Prize for Literature.

'Whatever the country, freedom of thought and expression are universal human rights.'

of repression is a moral necessity. Pamuk's remarks about the Kurds and Armenians were calculated to arouse a febrile national consciousness, but he spoke as a Turk convinced that his people had to confront certain facts, both historic and contemporary.

The Kurds were among the many nationalities seeking independence from the Ottoman Turkish empire, but their aspirations to independent statehood were frustrated. The empire's dissolution at the end of the First World War left the Kurds scattered across the contiguous boundaries of Iran, Iraq, Syria and the newly formed republic of Turkey. Conflict between the Turkish military and Kurdish secessionists has been intense in recent years, and use of the Kurdish language, legally prohibited by Turkey until 1991, remains subject to official restrictions. The First World War is also the background to the 'Armenian genocide': Ottoman Turkey, an Islamic culture, was at war with Russia, then still a Christian Orthodox civilization, and the Ottoman government suspected that the Christianity of its Armenian subjects inclined them to pro-Russian, and therefore treasonous, acts and sentiments. Neutral observers accept that between 1 and 1.5 million Armenians were killed between 1915 and 1917 as a result of an ethnic extermination authorized by the Ottoman imperial government. Pamuk was dealing with a 'forbidden topic', since the Turkish republic, as successor state to the Ottoman power, denied any such genocide. His concluding remarks may serve as a reminder why no one likes a missionary when he's armed.

In March 1985 Arthur Miller and Harold Pinter made a trip together to Istanbul. At the time, they were perhaps the two most important names in world theatre, but unfortunately it was not a play or literary event that brought them to Istanbul, but the limits being set on freedom of expression in Turkey . . . Whenever I've looked through the newspaper archives and the almanacs of that time . . . I soon come across the image that defines that era for most of us: men sitting in a courtroom, flanked by gendarmes, their heads shaven, frowning as their case proceeds. There were many writers among them, and Miller and Pinter had come to Istanbul to meet with them and their families, to offer them assistance, and to bring their plight to the attention of the world . . . A friend of mine and I were to be their guides . . .

Until then I had stood on the margins of the political world . . . but now, as I listened to suffocating tales of repression, cruelty and outright evil, I felt drawn to this world through guilt – drawn to it, too, by feelings of solidarity, but at the same time I felt an equal and opposite desire to protect myself from all this, and to do nothing in life but write beautiful novels . . .

I clearly remember one image: at one end of a very long corridor in the Istanbul Hilton, my friend and I are whispering to each other with some agitation, while at the other end, Miller and Pinter are whispering in the shadows with the same dark intensity. This image remained engraved in my troubled mind, I think, because it illustrated the great distance between our complicated histories and theirs, while suggesting at the same time that a consoling solidarity among writers was possible.

I felt the same sense of mutual pride and shared shame in every other meeting we attended . . . The writers, thinkers and journalists with whom we were meeting mostly defined themselves as leftists in those days . . . Twenty years on, when I see that half of these people – or thereabouts, I don't have the precise numbers – now align themselves with a nationalism that is at odds with Westernization and democracy, I of course feel sad . . .

Whatever the country, freedom of thought and expression are universal human rights. These freedoms, which modern people long for as much as bread and water, should never be limited by using nationalist sentiment, moral sensitivities or – worst of all – business or military interests . . . We must be alert to those who denigrate immigrants and minorities for their religion, their ethnic roots or the oppression that the governments of the countries they've left behind have visited on their own people.

'Our desire to understand those unlike us should never stand in the way of our respect for human rights'

But to respect the humanity and religious beliefs of minorities is not to suggest that we should limit freedom of thought . . . Our desire to understand those unlike us should never stand in the way of our respect for human rights.

I always have difficulty expressing my political judgements in a clear, emphatic and strong way – I feel pretentious, as if I'm saying things that are not quite true. This is because I know I cannot reduce my thoughts about life to the music of a single voice and a single point of view – I am, after all, a novelist, the kind of novelist who makes it his business to identify with all his characters, especially the bad ones. Living as I do in a world where, in a very short time, someone who has been a victim of tyranny and oppression can suddenly become one of the oppressors, I know also that holding strong beliefs about things and people is itself a difficult enterprise.

I do also believe that most of us entertain these contradictory thoughts simultaneously, in a spirit of good will and with the best of intentions. The pleasure of writing novels comes from exploring this peculiarly modern condition . . . we need to understand ourselves, our shady, contradictory, inner thoughts, and the pride and shame I mentioned earlier.

So let me tell another story that might cast some light on the shame and pride I felt 20 years ago while I was taking Miller and Pinter around Istanbul. In the ten years following their visit, a series of coincidences . . . led to my making a series of public statements on

*'Whatever the country, freedom of thought and expression are
universal human rights'*

freedom of expression that bore no relation to my novels, and before long I had taken on a political persona far more powerful than I had ever intended. It was at about this time that the Indian author of a United Nations report on freedom of expression . . . came to Istanbul and looked me up . . . He asked me a question that still echoes strangely in my mind: 'Mr Pamuk, what is there going on in your country that you would like to explore in your novels but shy away from, due to legal prohibitions?' . . .

'When another writer in another house is not free, no writer is free.'

In the Turkey of ten years ago, there were many more subjects kept closed by laws and oppressive state policies than there are today, but as I went through them one by one, I could find none that I wished to explore 'in my novels'. But I knew, nonetheless, that if I said 'there is nothing I wish to write in my novels that I am not able to discuss', I'd be giving the wrong impression. For I'd already begun to speak often and openly about all these dangerous subjects . . . As I thought all this through, I was at once ashamed of my silence, and reconfirmed in my belief that freedom of expression has its roots in pride, and is, in essence, an expression of human dignity. I have personally known writers who have chosen to raise forbidden topics purely because they were forbidden. I think I am no different. Because when another writer in another house is not free, no writer is free . . .

Sometimes my friends rightly tell me or someone else, 'You shouldn't have put it quite like that; if only you had worded it like this, in a way that no one would find offensive, you wouldn't be in so much trouble now.' But to change one's words and package them in a way that will be acceptable to everyone in a repressed culture . . . is shaming and degrading.

The theme of this year's PEN festival is reason and belief . . . So let us now ask ourselves how 'reasonable' it is to denigrate cultures and religions, or, more to the point, to mercilessly bomb countries, in the name of democracy and freedom of thought . . . In the war against Iraq, the tyrannization and heartless murder of almost 100,000 people has brought neither peace nor democracy. To the contrary, it has served to ignite nationalist, anti-Western anger. Things have become a great deal more difficult for the small minority who are struggling for democracy and secularism in the Middle East. This savage, cruel war is the shame of America and the West. Organizations like PEN and writers like Harold Pinter and Arthur Miller are its pride.

*'As of today, the time for denial,
the time for delay, has at last
come to an end'*

Kevin Rudd
(b. 1957)

THE AUSTRALIAN PRIME MINISTER APOLOGIZES TO HIS COUNTRY'S INDIGENOUS
PEOPLES FOR PAST WRONGS; CANBERRA, 13 FEBRUARY 2008

'As of today, the time for denial, the time for delay,
has at last come to an end'

By tabling a parliamentary motion expressing contrition for the ill-treatment of Australia's indigenous peoples, Kevin Rudd was fulfilling a campaign promise. Labour's recent election win on a 5.4 per cent swing was substantial, and that decisive shift towards the centre-left made him prime minister. Rudd promised 'a new style of leadership' and a reserved manner distinguished him from the Australian political tradition's frequent exuberance. His fluency in Mandarin and diplomatic expertise qualified Rudd to speak authoritatively on Australia's strategic relationship with China and southeast Asia, and in running for office he had stressed his practical experience as both bureaucrat and businessman. When he spoke of the 'stolen generations' to the House of Representatives, the premier's seriousness of purpose did justice to the issues raised by 'one of the darkest chapters in Australia's history'. But his speech also displayed an imaginative grasp of their significance for Australia's future as well as her past. 'This unfinished business' was a question of natural justice, and the apology was presented as the final stage in Australia's dismantling of colonial attitudes. The era which had started with the white man's arrival had finished, and Rudd was ushering in a more inclusive epoch.

The indigenous population of Australia is descended from migrants who arrived from Asia at least 50,000 years ago. The 'Dreaming', or 'Dreamtime', referred to by Rudd describes the sacred period which, according to these peoples' traditional lore, preceded the earth's creation and whose mythic values subsist in the symbols and beliefs of the present. Enforced separation of indigenous children from their parents was first adopted as a policy in Australia under the provisions adopted by the colony of Victoria under its Aboriginal Protection Act (1869). Other Australian states would adopt the same means to ensure a common goal: the eventual 'breeding out' of the original population to ensure its eventual genetic, and cultural, assimilation to the white majority. Rudd's apology was extended to

KEVIN RUDD (b. 1952)

1981 Graduates in Asian Studies from Australian National University, Canberra.

1981–8 Career diplomat, Department of Foreign Affairs.

1989–92 Chief of staff to the premier of Queensland, Wayne Goss (Labour).

1992–5 Director general of the Cabinet Office, government of Queensland.

1996–8 Senior China consultant to the accountancy firm KPMG Australia.

1998 Elected member of the House of Representatives, Parliament of Australia.

2001–5 Shadow minister for foreign affairs.

2006 Elected leader of the Australian Labour Party.

2007 Labour wins the federal election (24 Nov), defeating the incumbent Liberal–National Party coalition government; sworn in as prime minister (3 Dec).

include the indigenous population of the Torres Strait Islands, which lie between the northern Australian coast and New Guinea, and who were subjected to the same measures.

Late 20th-century statistics for illiteracy, ill health and unemployment among the indigenous population offered a tragic commentary on an original policy goal of social 'improvement'. The report of the national inquiry into the 'stolen generations', published in 1997 as 'Bringing Them Home', concluded that Australian legislatures should express an official apology for the forcible removals. The state parliaments of Victoria, South Australia and New South Wales, and the parliament of the Northern Territory, proceeded to do so. But the then prime minister John Howard rejected the idea of a federal government apology.

Howard's opposition was motivated partly by a career-long rejection of multiculturalism but also by a concern that the Australian government would face claims for financial compensation if it apologized. Speaking shortly before the 2007 election, he nonetheless recognized that 'the crisis of indigenous cultural and social disintegration requires a stronger affirmation of indigenous identity and culture'. Howard had sensed the public mood, but it was Rudd who represented the new empathy. The motion, supported by the Liberal official opposition, was adopted unanimously by both the House and the Senate.

I move: That today we honour the indigenous peoples of this land, the oldest continuing cultures in human history. We reflect on their past mistreatment. We reflect in particular on the mistreatment of those who were stolen generations – this blemished chapter in our nation's history . . .

We apologize for the laws and policies of successive parliaments and governments that have inflicted profound grief, suffering and loss on these our fellow Australians. We apologize especially for the removal of Aboriginal and Torres Strait Islander children from their families, their communities and their country.

For the pain, suffering and hurt of these stolen generations, their descendants and for their families left behind, we say sorry.

To the mothers and the fathers, the brothers and sisters, for the breaking-up of families and communities, we say sorry.

And for the indignity and degradation thus inflicted on a proud people and a proud culture, we say sorry.

We the parliament of Australia respectfully request that this apology be received in the spirit in which it is offered as part of the healing of the nation.

For the future we take heart; resolving that this new page in the history of our great continent can now be written . . .

'For the pain, suffering and hurt of these stolen generations, their descendants and for their families left behind, we say sorry'

There comes a time in the history of nations when their peoples must become fully reconciled to their past if they are to go forward with confidence to embrace their future.

Our nation, Australia, has reached such a time.

That is why this parliament is today here assembled: to deal with this unfinished business of the nation, to remove a great stain from the nation's soul and, in a true spirit of reconciliation, to open a new chapter in the history of this great land, Australia . . .

There has been a stony, stubborn and deafening silence for more than a decade; a view that somehow we, the parliament, should suspend our most basic instincts of what is right and what is wrong; a view that, instead, we should look for any pretext to push this great wrong to one side, to leave it languishing with the historians, the academics and the cultural warriors, as if the stolen generations are little more than an interesting sociological phenomenon.

'There comes a time in the history of nations when their peoples must become fully reconciled to their past'

But the stolen generations are not intellectual curiosities. They are human beings, human beings who have been damaged deeply by the decisions of parliaments and governments. But, as of today, the time for denial, the time for delay, has at last come to an end . . .

Should there still be doubts as to why we must now act, let the parliament reflect for a moment on the following facts: that, between 1910 and 1970, between 10 and 30 per cent of indigenous children were forcibly taken from their mothers and fathers; that, as a result, up to 50,000 children were forcibly taken from their families; that this was the product of the deliberate, calculated policies of the state as reflected in the explicit powers given to them under statute . . .

We must acknowledge these facts if we are to deal once and for all with the argument that the policy of a generic forced separation was somehow well motivated, justified by its historical context . . . Let us remember the fact that the forced removal of Aboriginal children was happening as late as the early 1970s . . . It is well within the adult memory span of many of us . . .

It is for these reasons . . . that the governments and parliaments of this nation must make this apology – because, put simply, the laws that our parliaments enacted made the stolen generations possible. We, the parliaments of this nation, are ultimately responsible, not those who gave effect to our laws. And the problem lay with the laws themselves.

As has been said of settler societies elsewhere, we are the bearers of many blessings from our ancestors; therefore we must also be the bearer of their burdens as well. Therefore, for our nation, the course of action is clear: that is, to deal now with what has become one of the darkest chapters in Australia's history.

In doing so . . . we are also wrestling with our own soul . . . Until we fully confront that truth, there will always be a shadow hanging over us and our future as a fully united and fully reconciled people . . .

To the stolen generations, I say the following: as prime minister of Australia, I am sorry. On behalf of the government of Australia, I am sorry . . . We apologize for the hurt, the pain and suffering that we, the parliament, have caused you by the laws that previous parliaments have enacted. We apologize for the indignity, the degradation and the humiliation these laws embodied. We offer this apology to the mothers, the fathers, the brothers, the sisters, the families and the communities whose lives were ripped apart by the actions of successive governments under successive parliaments . . .

Our challenge for the future is . . . to embrace a new partnership between indigenous and non-indigenous Australians . . . The core of this partnership for the future is to close the gap between indigenous and non-indigenous Australians on life expectancy, educational achievement and employment opportunities . . .

Let us . . . allow this day, this day of national reconciliation, to become one of those rare moments in which we might just be able to transform the way in which the nation thinks about itself, whereby the injustice administered to the stolen generations in the name of these, our parliaments, causes all of us to reappraise, at the deepest level of our beliefs, the real possibility of reconciliation writ large: reconciliation across all indigenous Australia; reconciliation across the entire history of the often bloody encounter between those who emerged from the Dreamtime a thousand generations ago and those who, like me, came across the seas only yesterday . . .

It is for the nation to bring the first two centuries of our settled history to a close, as we begin a new chapter. We embrace with pride, admiration and awe these great and ancient cultures we are truly blessed to have among us, cultures that provide a unique, uninterrupted human thread linking our Australian continent to the most ancient prehistory of our planet . . .

Let us . . . write this new chapter in our nation's story together.

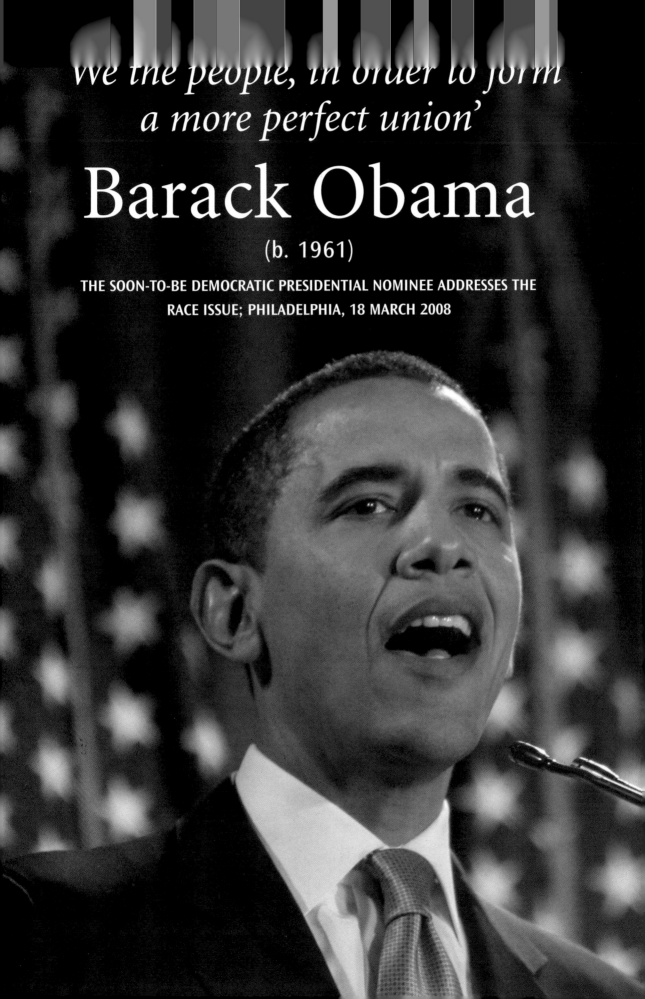

We the people, in order to form a more perfect union'

Barack Obama

(b. 1961)

THE SOON-TO-BE DEMOCRATIC PRESIDENTIAL NOMINEE ADDRESSES THE
RACE ISSUE; PHILADELPHIA, 18 MARCH 2008

Barack Obama's emergence as a politician of the first rank was an emotionally arousing moment in America's history, and the enthusiasm he engendered meant that the junior senator from Illinois became a figure of international significance while campaigning to become the Democratic nominee for the presidency. America's involvement in the Iraq War remained unpopular both at home and abroad during 2007–8, and Obama's consistent opposition to the war distinguished him from Senator Hillary Clinton, his chief rival for the nomination. Obama was the candidate of change, following the two-term presidency of George W. Bush, and his public statements sought to express 'the audacity of hope' – a phrase coined by his Chicago pastor, Jeremiah Wright. Those sentiments were delivered in the rich baritone timbre which distinguished Obama's soaring oratory, and the elegant equipoise of his cadences urged America towards a deepening of the union between her states and among her peoples.

During his campaign's earlier phase Obama had concentrated on the domestic policy questions which had arisen during a major economic downturn, and he had not drawn attention to the issue of race. He benefited from a widespread disenchantment with sectarian attitudes and divisive policies, and the large sums of money he raised for his campaign through the internet showed his grasp of how technology could transform traditional politics. Obama's origins and upbringing were central to his candidacy as a different kind of politician, but his personal manner was reserved in its dignity and instinctively intellectual.

BARACK OBAMA (b. 1961)

1983 Graduates from Columbia University, New York City.

1985–8 Director of Developing Communities Project, Chicago.

1988–91 Harvard Law School; edits (1990) *Harvard Law Review*.

1992–2004 Lecturer at University of Chicago Law School.

1993 Joins the law firm Davis, Miner, Barnhill and Galland, and becomes a counsel (1996–2004).

1995 Publishes *Dreams from My Father: A Story of Race and Inheritance*.

1996 Elected to the Illinois Senate; subsequently re-elected (1998, 2002); resigns seat in Nov 2004.

July 2004 Delivers keynote address to the Democratic Party national convention; elected (Nov) to US Senate.

2006 *The Audacity of Hope: Thoughts on Reclaiming the American Dream.*

Feb 2007 Announces candidacy to become the Democratic nominee in the 2008 presidential election.

3 June 2008 Becomes the Democratic presumptive nominee.

'We the people, in order to form a more perfect union'

Born in Honolulu and partly raised in Jakarta after his mother's remarriage to an Indonesian national, Obama conformed to few stereotypes, and an Ivy League education distinguished him from the previous generation of African-American politicians. His involvement in community-based projects, initially as a professional and then as a volunteer, demonstrated Obama's seriousness about extending opportunity among the disadvantaged – both black and white – through civic-based activism. Until the spring of 2008, however, his presidential campaigning encouraged the idea that race was an issue to be transcended rather than dwelt upon, and his life story was presented as being exemplary in that regard. A more direct discussion of race became necessary after ABC broadcast excerpts from sermons preached by the Reverend Jeremiah Wright at the Trinity United Church of Christ in Chicago, where Obama had been a member for many years. Wright was Obama's close personal friend as well as his pastor, and those sentences in the sermons which expressed racially charged opinions threatened to expose the candidate to accusations of having concealed his true views.

Obama's response was delivered in Philadelphia, where the Federal Convention had met in 1787 to draft the US constitution, and his emphasis on a union which was a continuing process rather than an achieved event was both intellectually acute and emotionally persuasive. The candidate for a more inclusive America confirmed his moral authority and retained his political appeal. Wright claimed weeks later that the Philadelphia speech was mere political positioning, and on 29 April 2008 Obama disowned his former pastor.

'We the people, in order to form a more perfect union.'

Two hundred and twenty-one years ago in a hall that still stands across the street, a group of men gathered and, with these simple words, launched America's improbable experiment in democracy . . . The document they produced was eventually signed but ultimately unfinished. It was stained by this nation's original sin of slavery, a question that divided the colonies and brought the convention to a stalemate until the founders chose . . . to leave any final resolution to future generations.

Of course, the answer to the slavery question was already embedded within our constitution – a constitution that had at its very core the ideal of equal citizenship . . . And yet words on a parchment would not be enough to deliver slaves from bondage, or provide men and women of every colour and creed their full rights and obligations as citizens of the United States. What would be needed were Americans in successive generations who were willing . . . to narrow that gap between the promise of our ideals and the reality of their time . . .

'I will never forget that in no other country on earth is my story even possible'

Quercus Publishing Plc
21 Bloomsbury Square
London
WC1A 2NS

First published in 2009

A catalogue record of this book is available from the British Library

Cloth case edition
ISBN 978 1 84724 836 7

Printed case edition
ISBN 978 1 84866 014 4

Paperback with flaps
ISBN 978 184724 919 7

Editor: Ben Dupré
Designer: Patrick Nugent
Picture researcher: Claudia Tate

Printed and bound in China

10 9 8 7 6 5 4 3 2 1